LIVING WITH ADULT AUTISM

PRACTICAL TOOLS FOR EXECUTIVE FUNCTIONING, SENSORY OVERLOAD, AND BETTER COMMUNICATION, SO YOU CAN THRIVE UNMASKED

CLAUDE MOORE

CONTENTS

Introduction   5

1. Understanding and Embracing Your Autistic
   Identity   7
2. Sensory Management and Overload   19
3. Enhancing Communication and Social Skills   31
4. Navigating Professional Life   45
5. Self-Care and Mental Health   57
6. Building Community and Support Networks   71
7. Practical Daily Living Skills   83
8. Empowerment and Advocacy   95
9. Embracing Neurodiversity in a Neurotypical World   109

   Conclusion   125
   References   129

INTRODUCTION

A few years ago, I attended a conference on autism. As I sat in the bustling room, I noticed a man standing off to the side. He seemed overwhelmed by the noise and activity. After the session, I approached him and we began to talk. His name was David, and he shared with me his struggles with navigating the chaos of daily life. He had challenges with executive functioning and often felt trapped in a world that moved too fast for him. Yet, he had a keen mind and a passion for art. Our conversation stayed with me, shaping the core of this book.

The purpose of this book is clear. It is a practical and supportive handbook for adults with autism. It focuses on overcoming challenges like executive functioning and sensory overload. This book aims to help you navigate your world with more ease and confidence.

My vision is to empower you to live your life authentically. I want to provide you with practical tools and strategies, which will help you optimize daily life. Living authentically means embracing who you are and feeling comfortable in your own skin. It means having the tools to navigate the world while staying true to yourself.

You, the reader, may face unique challenges each day. Whether it's the sensory overload of a crowded room or the complexity of social interactions, these challenges are real and significant. You deserve strategies and support tailored to your experiences.

This book is specifically for autistic adults. Many autism resources are aimed at children, but adults have different needs and experiences. This book includes diverse voices and experiences. It reflects a wide range of perspectives, offering insights that resonate with adults in a variety of different categories.

Consider these statistics: about 1 in 54 adults are on the autism spectrum, according to recent studies. Many face challenges in employment, relationships, and daily living. This book seeks to address those challenges with practical, evidence-based strategies. It is grounded in research and informed by real-life experiences.

The book is structured into chapters that each address a specific area of life. We will begin with understanding sensory processing and move onto executive functioning. Communication and social relationships will also be key areas of focus. Each chapter offers practical advice and strategies you can apply immediately.

As you read, you can expect to gain practical strategies and validation of your experiences. You will find empowerment in the tools and ideas presented. This book is a guide to help you thrive unmasked, living your life in a way that feels right for you.

I invite you to join me on this journey of self-discovery and empowerment. Together, we will explore the strategies and tools that can help you live a fulfilling life. Let us begin this journey with the knowledge that you are not alone and that living authentically is within your reach.

ONE
UNDERSTANDING AND EMBRACING YOUR AUTISTIC IDENTITY

When I first met Roxy, she was hesitant to join the conversation. We stood in a quiet corner of a bustling conference, and she confided in me about her recent autism diagnosis. In her words, it felt like unlocking a door to a room that had always been there, but one she could now explore with understanding. This newfound insight allowed her to connect the dots of her experiences, from childhood to adulthood, in ways that finally made sense. Her story is a testament to the profound impact of self-discovery and acceptance, which is at the heart of this chapter. Understanding and embracing your autistic identity is a journey of self-awareness, reflection, and growth. For many adults, this means recognizing and appreciating the unique aspects of autism that make you who you are. This chapter aims to guide you through the process of self-discovery, providing insights and strategies to help you navigate your identity confidently, and with clarity.

1.1 DISCOVERING YOUR AUTISTIC SELF

The autism spectrum is vast and diverse, as unique as each individual who identifies with it. Embracing this diversity is fundamental to understanding your own identity. Autistic traits—such as sensory sensitivities, distinct communication preferences, and focused interests—are not limitations but aspects of your individuality that enrich your experiences.

It is vital to dispel common misconceptions, like the notion that autistic people lack empathy or creativity. Many autistic individuals possess exceptional emotional depth and innovative thinking, challenging these outdated stereotypes.

Reflecting on your own experiences can be a powerful way to understand your autistic self. Journaling, for instance, provides a private space to document and explore your thoughts and feelings. As you write, you may begin to identify patterns in your behavior and experiences that highlight your strengths and challenges. Recognizing how your traits influence your interactions and perceptions can help you appreciate the unique ways you engage with the world.

Building self-knowledge is a key step in embracing your autistic identity. Seek out information and resources that resonate with you, whether through books, websites, or community groups. Connecting with others on your path can provide invaluable support. Autistic communities, whether online or in person, offer spaces of shared understanding and mutual encouragement. Here, you can learn from others' experiences while contributing your own insights. This exploration is an opportunity to define what being autistic means to you in a personal and meaningful way.

In this chapter, we embark on a journey of self-discovery, highlighting the importance of understanding and embracing your autistic identity. Through reflection, exploration, and connection, you can gain the tools and insights needed to live authentically and confidently as an autistic adult. This process is not about changing who you are but about recognizing and celebrating the unique qualities that make you, you.

1.2 NAVIGATING A LATE DIAGNOSIS

Receiving an autism diagnosis later in life can be a profoundly emotional experience, one that stirs a complex mix of feelings. It often arrives after years of grappling with unanswered questions and a sense of difference from those around you. Many adults find themselves looking back at their lives, seeing the past through a new lens. This revelation can bring a profound sense of relief, as if finally having the right words to describe a familiar but elusive feeling. Yet, it often comes with disbelief or uncertainty. The realization that these traits, which have shaped so many aspects of your life, are part of a recognized condition can be both comforting and overwhelming. The initial reaction might include relief, knowing there is a valid explanation for the struggles you've faced. For others, there's a period of mourning for the years spent without understanding. Understanding these emotions is vital, as they are a natural part of integrating this new aspect into your sense of self.

Incorporating a late diagnosis into your identity can be an empowering process of reframing your life experiences. It offers a chance to reevaluate past experiences with the clarity of hindsight. What once were perceived as personal failings might now be understood as traits of autism. This shift can lead to self-compassion and acceptance. Instead of seeing challenges as isolated incidents, you can recognize them as part of a broader pattern. This awareness allows you to rewrite your narrative, transforming past struggles into a tapestry of resilience and adaptability. Finding validation in your experiences helps you to embrace this aspect of your identity. The diagnosis doesn't change who you are but provides a framework to understand yourself more fully. By integrating this knowledge, you open the door to self-discovery and acceptance.

Discussing a late diagnosis with family and friends can be daunting. These conversations involve crafting a personal narrative that resonates with your truth while setting clear boundaries and expectations. They are an opportunity to educate those close to you about what autism means in your life, and they can help dispel misconceptions and encourage empathy and support. You have the right to define your comfort level in sharing details of your diagnosis. This dialogue is not just about informing others but also about creating a supportive environment where your authentic self is acknowledged and valued.

Seeking support and resources can be very helpful after a late diagnosis. Autistic support groups, both online and in person, offer spaces for shared stories and practical advice. Professional counseling with autism-informed therapists can also help you process your diagnosis and integrate it into your sense of self. Together, these tools provide a foundation for navigating your identity with confidence and clarity.

Reflection Section: Crafting Your Narrative

One useful tool is to reflect on how to share your diagnosis with others. Consider writing a personal narrative that captures your journey. Think about key experiences that shaped your understanding of yourself. How has your diagnosis provided clarity or relief? What boundaries are important for you to establish in conversations with loved ones? Use this narrative as a guide when discussing your diagnosis, ensuring your story is told in a way that respects your journey and promotes understanding.

Navigating a late autism diagnosis involves embracing a multifaceted process of self-discovery, dialogue, and connection. Each individual's path is unique, defined by personal insights and the support systems they build. Understanding the emotional landscape of a late diagnosis can help you integrate this aspect into your identity, leading to a deeper understanding and acceptance of who you are.

1.3 THE POWER OF SELF-ACCEPTANCE IN AUTISM

Embracing neurodiversity isn't just a concept; it is a call to recognize and celebrate the inherent value of diverse neurological makeups, including autism. This movement challenges the conventional views that often pathologize differences, instead advocating for a paradigm shift that sees these differences as essential to the rich landscape of humanity. By embracing neurodiversity, we acknowledge that every mind offers unique perspectives and insights, contributing to human thought and experience diversity. The benefits of this acceptance are profound: it fosters a society that values varied cognitive styles, encouraging innovation and empathy. When we embrace our differences, we open doors to new ways of thinking and living, enriching our collective human experience.

Building self-confidence starts with self-acceptance. Positive affirmations and self-talk can be powerful tools in this process. By consciously choosing to affirm your strengths and capabilities, you challenge the internal voice that may have been conditioned by years of misunderstanding or stigma. Telling yourself, "I am capable," or "My perspective is valuable," can become a mantra that slowly reshapes your internal dialogue. Celebrating personal achievements, no matter how small, further reinforces this self-belief. Whether it's mastering a new skill or simply navigating a challenging day, recognizing these successes builds a foundation of confidence. This celebration of achievements not only acknowledges your efforts but also honors your unique contributions to the world.

Overcoming internalized stigma requires a conscious effort to challenge and replace negative beliefs with self-compassion. Stigma can often manifest as self-doubt or feelings of inadequacy rooted in societal misconceptions about autism. To combat this, start by identifying these negative beliefs and actively question their validity. Are they based on fact, or are they remnants of outdated stereotypes? Replace these thoughts with self-compassion, reminding yourself that being different is not a deficiency. Embrace the idea that your experiences and perspectives are valid and valuable. This shift in mindset can lead to a more compassionate view of yourself, which in turn can lead to greater resilience and a sense of belonging.

Role models can also play a significant role in shaping how we perceive ourselves. Seeing influential autistic individuals who have embraced their identities can be incredibly inspiring. Figures like Temple Grandin and John Elder Robison have used their platforms to advocate for autism awareness and acceptance, demonstrating the power of authenticity. Their biographies and personal accounts provide a narrative of strength and perseverance, offering a beacon of hope and possibility. Such public figures impact self-perception by showing that it is not only possible to succeed as an autistic individual but that one's unique traits can be a source of strength and innovation. Their stories remind us that embracing our true selves can lead to extraordinary achievements, inspiring others to do the same.

In the tapestry of self-acceptance, each thread is woven with intention and care. Embracing neurodiversity, building self-confidence, overcoming stigma, and drawing inspiration from role models are all integral to this process. They serve as guiding lights on the path to understanding and accepting yourself wholly, creating a life that is not only authentic but also deeply fulfilling. These efforts not only empower ourselves but also contribute to a broader culture that values and celebrates diversity in all its forms.

1.4 UNMASKING: EMBRACING AUTHENTICITY

For many autistic individuals, masking has been a mechanism for navigating a world that often feels at odds with their natural state. Masking involves adopting behaviors that align with societal norms, such as forcing eye contact or mimicking typical speech patterns, all in an effort to blend in and avoid negative attention. This adaptation is often driven by social pressures and the need to conform in environments that may not fully understand or accept neurodiverse behaviors. While masking might offer a temporary sense of safety or acceptance, its long-term consequences can be profound. Chronic masking requires immense cognitive and emotional energy, leading to exhaustion and a disconnection from one's true self. Over time, the weight of masking can culminate in feelings of isolation, anxiety, and even depression. Understanding these dynamics is crucial as you consider the path to authenticity.

Embracing your authentic self starts with the gradual process of unmasking. This involves identifying specific situations where you feel the urge to mask, such as social gatherings or professional settings. Recognizing these triggers allows you to develop strategies for handling them more authentically. Begin by practicing authenticity in safe environments where you feel supported and accepted. This might be with trusted friends or within communities that celebrate neurodiversity. Allow yourself to express your natural traits without fear of judgment or reprisal. As you grow more comfortable, extend this practice to broader contexts, gradually reducing the need for masking. This process is not about forcing change but gently allowing your true self to surface.

The benefits of embracing authenticity are far-reaching. As you align your external actions with your internal self, you may experience increased personal satisfaction. Living authentically can enhance your sense of self-worth and reduce the mental strain associated with maintaining a facade. Furthermore, authenticity is closely tied to improved mental health. Reducing the need for constant vigilance and self-monitoring frees up cognitive resources, decreasing anxiety and stress. Authentic living also fosters stronger personal relationships. When you present your true self to others, it invites genuine connection and understanding. Relationships built on authenticity are often more meaningful and resilient as they are based on mutual acceptance and respect. As you embrace your authenticity, it becomes a source of strength and resilience, which will have a positive effect on your experience of life.

Creating safe spaces for authenticity is an essential component of this process. Surrounding yourself with supportive friends and communities is vital. These are individuals and groups who understand and value your unique traits, offering encouragement and acceptance. Open communication is another benefit of authenticity. By creating an environment where open dialogue is encouraged, you develop a foundation of trust and understanding. This involves actively listening to others and sharing your own experiences and needs. Establishing clear communication strategies can help bridge gaps and promote empathy, ensuring that your authentic self is met with acceptance. Encouraging open conversations about neurodiversity can also contribute to creating inclusive environments where authenticity is celebrated. As you build these spaces, you cultivate an environment where your true self can flourish without fear of judgment or rejection.

In my own life, I've seen how transformative unmasking can be. One friend, Alex, told me how they've always felt the need to suppress their hand flapping in public. Over time, they began practicing their natural stimming behaviors in private settings, gradually gaining the confidence to allow these movements in public. Initially, Alex feared negative reactions but found that those who mattered were accepting and supportive. This authenticity allowed Alex to connect more deeply with themselves and others, reducing the anxiety associated with constant self-censorship. This experience highlights the profound impact of embracing one's authentic self and the importance of creating environments that support this authenticity.

Embracing authenticity is not merely about shedding masks but about nurturing a self that is free to be genuine. It is a process that requires courage and vulnerability, but the rewards are significant. By understanding masking and taking steps towards unmasking, you can unlock a life that is richer and more aligned with who you truly are. As you explore this path, each step toward authenticity brings you closer to a sense of belonging and fulfillment that enhances every aspect of your life.

1.5 INTERSECTIONALITY: GENDER, RACE, AND AUTISM

The concept of intersectionality is an essential component of understanding the complex realities faced by autistic individuals. This framework, which examines how various social identities intersect, is crucial in autism research and advocacy. It helps us appreciate how factors like gender, race, and culture shape the autistic experience. By recognizing these layers, we can better understand the unique challenges that arise when these identities intertwine. For instance, an autistic person who is also navigating societal expectations related to gender or race faces distinct hurdles. These intersectional challenges demand a nuanced approach that considers the full spectrum of an individual's identity.

Gender identity plays a significant role in how people experience autism. Non-binary and transgender autistic individuals often encounter additional layers of complexity. Society's expectations around gender can amplify the challenges of autism, requiring individuals to navigate not only the intricacies of social interactions but also the pressures associated with gender norms. For example, an autistic person who is non-binary might struggle with societal gender expectations that feel restrictive or misaligned with their identity. This can impact how they express themselves and interact with others. In these cases, the intersection of autism and gender identity can lead to both unique challenges and strengths. The more we understand and support these experiences, the greater inclusivity we may experience.

Race and cultural identity also profoundly influence the autistic experience. Cultural perceptions of autism vary widely, influencing how individuals are perceived and treated within their communities. Navigating these cultural expectations can be challenging, as it often involves balancing personal identity with social norms. The representation of diverse voices in autism discussions is critical to expanding our understanding of these experiences. By including a range of cultural perspectives, we can challenge stereotypes and promote more inclusive narratives. This representation is not just beneficial—it is necessary to ensure that all voices are heard and valued.

As we reflect on these intersectional dynamics, it's clear that understanding autism requires a commitment to inclusivity and diversity. By acknowledging the roles of gender, race, and culture, we can create a more supportive and empathetic environment for all autistic individuals. This approach not only enriches our understanding of autism but also strengthens the bonds within our communities. Embracing intersectionality allows us to see individuals in their entirety, celebrating the unique contributions each brings to the world. In this way, we move towards a future where every voice is heard and valued, creating a world that is more inclusive and accepting of all identities.

TWO
SENSORY MANAGEMENT AND OVERLOAD

I magine walking through a bustling city street. The honking of cars, the chattering of pedestrians, and the glare of digital bill-boards combine into a cacophony that can feel like a tidal wave crashing over you. For many autistic adults, this overwhelming experience isn't occasional—it's a frequent reality. It can be overwhelming and exhausting, affecting how you interact with the world around you. Sensory overload can profoundly impact daily life, but understanding these experiences can help you navigate them with greater awareness and control. This chapter explores sensory processing and offers strategies to manage sensory challenges better.

2.1 UNDERSTANDING SENSORY PROCESSING IN AUTISM

Sensory processing is the way our brains interpret and respond to sensory inputs from the environment. For autistic individuals, this process often differs significantly from the neurotypical experience. The interpretation of sensory input—whether visual, auditory, tactile, or otherwise—can be heightened or dulled, impacting everyday activities. You might find that certain sounds are unbearably loud or that textures that others find pleasant are intensely uncomfortable. This heightened sensitivity can lead to sensory overload, resulting in stress and anxiety as your brain tries to process too much information at once. Conversely, you might also experience hyposensitivity, where certain stimuli are underwhelming, leading you to seek out more intense sensory experiences in order to feel engaged or centered.

Sensory sensitivities in autism often fall into two categories: hypersensitivity and hyposensitivity. Hypersensitivity means that your senses are overly acute, where a simple aroma might be overpowering, or a gentle touch feels like a jolt. Common triggers for hypersensitivity include bright lights, loud noises, and strong smells. You may find that you instinctively withdraw from these stimuli to avoid discomfort. On the other hand, hyposensitivity involves a reduced perception of sensory input. In this case, you might seek out intense sensations, such as preferring spicy foods or engaging in repetitive motions like rocking. These sensory-seeking behaviors are ways to fulfill a need for more sensory input, helping you achieve a sense of balance or comfort.

The scientific community has proposed various theories to explain the sensory differences observed in autism. One prominent theory is sensory integration theory, which suggests that individuals with autism process sensory information differently due to neurological variations. These differences can affect how the brain organizes and uses sensory information, leading to the unique sensory experiences you might encounter. Research also points to variations in sensory pathways in the brain, suggesting that the way neurons communicate in autistic individuals may differ from neurotypical patterns. Understanding these neurological differences provides insights into why sensory processing can feel so distinct and sometimes challenging, offering a foundation for strategies to manage these experiences.

Recognizing your personal sensory profile will help you to manage your sensory experiences better. This involves identifying your sensory preferences and sensitivities, which can vary significantly from person to person. Self-assessment tools can be invaluable in this process, helping you pinpoint specific stimuli that affect you positively or negatively. By noting your reactions to different sensory inputs, you can begin to map out a comprehensive picture of your sensory landscape. Keeping a sensory diary is a great way to help you understand your sensory experiences and the contexts in which they occur. Documenting your sensory experiences over time will help you see patterns. That, in turn, will reveal insights into how best to manage your sensory environment.

Sensory Profile Reflection Exercise

Set aside a few minutes each day to reflect on your sensory experiences. Note any particular sights, sounds, or textures that stood out and how they made you feel. Did certain stimuli cause discomfort or calmness? Observe the patterns that emerge, offering insights into your sensory preferences. This awareness allows you to make adjustments to your environment, creating spaces that support your comfort and well-being.

2.2 CREATING SENSORY-FRIENDLY SPACES AT HOME

Your home should be a sanctuary, a place where you feel secure and at ease. Designing a sensory-friendly environment involves thoughtful choices that cater to your unique sensory needs. Start by considering the colors and textures in each room. Calming colors like soft blues, muted greens, and gentle lavenders can create a serene atmosphere, reducing visual stress and promoting relaxation. Textures play a crucial role, too. Soft fabrics and smooth surfaces provide comfort, while rough or scratchy materials are best avoided. Lighting is also important. Adjustable lighting options, such as dimmer switches and warm LED bulbs, allow you to control the intensity and color of light according to your comfort. This control can be especially beneficial during different times of the day, helping you transition from the bright energy of morning to the soothing calm of evening.

Organizing your space into sensory zones is another way to enhance your comfort and well-being. Consider creating specific areas tailored to different sensory needs. Create a quiet zone for relaxation and decompression. This might be a cozy corner with soft pillows and blankets where you can retreat when the world feels overwhelming. It's a place for solitude, reflection, and recharging. Obviously, you can tailor this to your individual preferences. On the other hand, a stimulating zone is helpful when you seek sensory input. It could include a small area with vibrant colors, interactive toys, or a sound system for music that energizes you. Multi-purpose sensory corners are also beneficial. These versatile spaces can adapt to your needs, serving as a quiet zone one moment and a stimulating area the next. Flexibility in your environment allows you to respond to your sensory needs as they shift throughout the day.

There are quite a lot of sensory tools and aids available at this point in history, which can be helpful in enhancing your sensory comfort. Weighted blankets are a popular choice, providing deep pressure that can help calm your nervous system. They're perfect for moments when you need grounding and relaxation. Noise-cancelling headphones are another valuable tool, offering relief from overwhelming auditory stimuli. Whether it's the neighbor's

lawn mower or the hum of household appliances, these headphones create a bubble of silence, allowing you to focus or relax
without distraction. Aromatherapy diffusers can also play a role in
creating a sensory-friendly atmosphere. Scents like lavender or
chamomile promote relaxation, while citrus or peppermint
provide a refreshing burst of energy. Take time to find the right
combination of tools that work for you.

Establishing routines can also aid in maintaining a sensory-
friendly space. Consistent daily schedules provide a sense of
predictability and control, reducing anxiety and helping you
manage sensory input more effectively. For example, setting aside
designated times for sensory activities, such as a morning meditation or an evening reading session, can help you maintain balance
and well-being. Routines create structure in your day, allowing
you to anticipate and prepare for sensory experiences. This preparation can reduce the impact of unexpected stimuli, making your
environment feel more manageable. By integrating these routines
into your daily life, you build a foundation of stability that
supports your sensory needs.

Consider the layout and organization of your home as well.
Cluttered spaces can contribute to visual and mental overload,
making it harder to relax. Keeping your environment organized
and clutter-free can promote a sense of calm and order. Use
storage solutions that suit your style and needs, such as clear bins
or labeled shelves, to keep items accessible yet tidy. This organization supports your routines and helps maintain a sensory-friendly
environment. Your home should be a place that nurtures and
supports you, adapting to your sensory needs with ease and flexibility.

2.3 TECHNIQUES FOR REDUCING OVERLOAD IN THE WORKPLACE

Navigating the sensory landscape of a workplace can be challenging. The constant hum of office chatter, the flickering of fluorescent lights, and the open-plan design where personal space feels like a luxury can be overwhelming. These elements, seemingly innocuous to some, can pose significant challenges to autistic individuals, leading to sensory overload. Identifying these workplace triggers is the first step in managing them effectively. Noise is a common culprit; whether it's the persistent buzz of printers or the clatter of keyboards, these sounds can become a cacophony that disrupts focus. Lighting also plays a crucial role. Harsh, bright lights can intensify discomfort, making it difficult to concentrate. Not to mention, crowded or open office layouts can strip away privacy, increasing anxiety and stress. Recognizing these triggers is vital in forming strategies to minimize their impact on your workday.

Developing effective coping strategies will help you to create a more manageable work environment. Scheduled sensory breaks can offer respite from overwhelming stimuli, allowing you to step away and recharge. These breaks might include a quiet walk outside or a few moments in a designated quiet room, providing the necessary pause to reset your senses. Strategic seating arrangements can also help mitigate sensory challenges. If possible, choose a spot away from high-traffic areas or loud equipment. Facing away from bright lights or installing desk partitions can create a more controlled sensory space. These adjustments, though minor, can significantly enhance your comfort and productivity, reducing the likelihood of sensory overload.

In order to create a supportive work environment, you will likely need to communicate your sensory needs to your employer. Understanding your needs and how they impact your work is the first step to preparing for this conversation. Approach your supervisor with clear examples of how certain stimuli affect your performance. Requesting reasonable accommodations, such as noise-canceling headphones or adjustable lighting, can make a significant difference. Many employers are willing to accommodate these requests once they understand their necessity. For example, some individuals have successfully negotiated flexible working hours to avoid peak office noise or secured a quiet workspace away from the main office area. These accommodations not only improve your work experience but also demonstrate your proactive approach to managing your needs.

Building a supportive network within the workplace is also a helpful step for long-term success. Educating coworkers about sensory processing can open dialogues that promote empathy. Sharing experiences and discussing sensory challenges can demystify these issues, encouraging colleagues to be more considerate of your needs. Creating an inclusive workplace culture involves more than just individual efforts; it requires a collective understanding and respect for diversity. Encourage open conversations about sensory needs by suggesting a workplace seminar or presentation on neurodiversity. These initiatives can lay the groundwork for a more inclusive and accommodating work environment, benefiting not only you but also others who may have similar needs.

2.4 ADAPTIVE TOOLS FOR SENSORY CHALLENGES

Living with sensory sensitivities often means adapting your environment to better fit your unique needs. Thankfully, a variety of sensory tools exist to help manage these sensitivities, offering both relief and enhancement to your day-to-day life. Fidget spinners and stress balls are popular tools that provide tactile stimulation, helping to soothe and focus the mind. These items are small, portable, and can be used discreetly in various settings, making them convenient allies in moments of stress or distraction. Visual timers are another valuable tool, especially for managing time-related anxiety. These devices offer a clear visual representation of time passing, which can aid in planning and executing tasks without the pressure of traditional clocks. Using tools such as these can be a simple yet effective way to navigate sensory challenges, providing a sense of control and comfort.

Selecting the right sensory tools involves personally exploring your preferences and comfort levels. What works for one person might not work for another, so it's essential to consider what feels best for you. Start by identifying the specific sensory challenges you face and think about what types of input you find soothing or stimulating. A trial-and-error approach can be helpful here. Experiment with different tools to see which ones best meet your needs. If a fidget spinner feels too distracting, a stress ball may offer the right amount of feedback. If visual timers seem too rigid, you might try apps that provide more flexibility in tracking time. Remember, the goal is to find tools that enhance your well-being and fit seamlessly into your routine, offering support when and where you need it most.

Technology plays an increasingly important role in sensory management. In addition to the journaling mentioned previously, apps now exist that are designed for sensory tracking, helping you monitor your sensory experiences and providing insights into patterns and triggers. These apps often allow you to log sensory inputs and your reactions to them, creating a valuable record that can inform your strategies for managing sensitivities. Wearable technology is another innovative development in this field. Devices that offer sensory feedback, such as vibrating wristbands or pressure vests, can provide calming sensations in moments of stress.

These tools are designed to offer discreet support, allowing you to manage sensory challenges without drawing undue attention to yourself. Embracing technology in sensory management can open new avenues for understanding and adapting to your sensory world, offering tools that are both practical and empowering.

For those who enjoy creative projects, DIY sensory solutions can be a fulfilling way to address sensory needs. Crafting your own sensory aids allows you to customize and personalize them. Sensory bottles, for example, are simple to make and can be tailored to your preferences. Fill a clear bottle with water, glitter, or tiny beads, and watch as the contents swirl and settle, providing a calming visual experience. Textured cushions are another DIY project that can enhance your sensory environment. Choose fabrics that have textures you find soothing, such as soft fleece or nubby knits, and create cushions to place in areas where you relax. These homemade solutions not only offer sensory support but also provide a sense of accomplishment and creativity, turning the management of sensory challenges into a personalized and enjoyable endeavor.

As you explore these tools and technologies, consider keeping a journal or a list of what works for you. Documenting your experiences with different sensory aids can help you refine your approach and ensure that the tools you use are genuinely beneficial. Whether you choose commercially available products, embrace technological advancements, or create your own sensory solutions, the key is to prioritize comfort and ease. Integrating these tools into your daily life can help you reduce the incidence of sensory challenges. This exploration is about finding what resonates with you and creating a toolkit that empowers you to gain mastery over your sensory makeup confidently and comfortably.

2.5 SENSORY STRATEGIES FOR PUBLIC SPACES

Navigating public spaces can often feel like stepping into a whirl-wind of sensory input. The key to managing these experiences lies in preparation and awareness. Planning ahead for outings can make all the difference. Begin by researching sensory-friendly venues that accommodate diverse needs. Many places, such as museums or theaters, offer special hours or designated areas with reduced noise and lighting. Knowing which venues provide these options can help you plan your visit with confidence. Additionally, packing a sensory toolkit tailored to your personal preferences can be invaluable. Consider including noise-cancelling headphones or earbuds, sunglasses, or a favorite fidget tool. These items can offer comfort and stability in unpredictable environments, providing a sense of security as you venture into the world.

Having sensory strategies at hand is a big help when encountering crowded areas. For example, when entering a crowded space, identify quiet areas where you can take a break if needed. Many public places, such as shopping malls or parks, have designated quiet rooms or less frequented areas that can serve as temporary retreats. Even sitting somewhere off to the side for a few moments can provide a sensory break. Utilizing sensory distractions, such as listening to calming music or engaging with a tactile object, can also help divert your attention from overwhelming stimuli. These distractions provide a focal point, allowing you to ground yourself amidst the sensory chaos. By having a plan in place, you can approach crowded areas with greater assurance, knowing you have the tools necessary to manage your sensory experience.

Whether for leisure or necessity, travel presents its own sensory challenges. To minimize discomfort during transit, consider using noise-canceling headphones, especially on public transportation. These headphones, which now come in various earbud-type styles, can help drown out intrusive sounds, offering a semblance of peace in otherwise noisy environments. Planning your route ahead of time with sensory-friendly options in mind can also help. Choose routes that avoid peak hours or opt for quieter modes of transportation when possible. Furthermore, utilizing travel applications for planning can streamline your journey, providing real-time updates and reducing stress. These apps can help you anticipate delays or changes, ensuring that your travel experience is as smooth and predictable as possible.

Engaging in community activities is an important aspect of social life, yet it can be daunting for those sensitive to sensory input. To participate with minimal stress, seek out sensory-friendly events specifically designed to accommodate diverse needs. These events often feature modified environments, with adjustments to lighting and sound levels, making them more accessible. Gradual exposure to new environments can also help build your confidence over time. Start with smaller gatherings or familiar settings, gradually working your way up to larger events. This incremental approach allows you to acclimate to different stimuli at your own pace, reducing anxiety and increasing your comfort level. By taking these steps, you can enjoy community activities without feeling overwhelmed.

Throughout this chapter, we've explored various strategies to manage sensory experiences in different settings. From planning outings to engaging in community activities, the focus has been on equipping you with practical tools and insights to navigate sensory challenges. As we move forward, these foundational practices will support you in enhancing communication and social skills, helping you connect more deeply with the world around you.

THREE
ENHANCING COMMUNICATION AND SOCIAL SKILLS

When I first met Daniela, she was struggling to express her needs to those closest to her. Navigating the intricate dance of communication often felt like an insurmountable challenge. She shared how her family would sometimes misinterpret the absence of eye contact as disinterest or her direct speech as bluntness. Daniela's story highlights a common struggle for many autistic adults: bridging the communication gap with loved ones. Misunderstandings often arise when differences in nonverbal cues, emotional expression, or social expectations are interpreted through a neurotypical lens. This chapter explores strategies to enhance communication skills and engender meaningful connections with family and friends.

3.1 COMMUNICATION WITH LOVED ONES

Expressing needs to loved ones can be fraught with challenges, particularly when communication barriers arise. For autistic individuals, nonverbal cues such as facial expressions or gestures may be misinterpreted, leading to misunderstandings. Loved ones might misread a lack of eye contact as a sign of disengagement or assume that directness equates to harshness. Emotional regulation difficulties can further complicate interactions. You may find it challenging to articulate feelings when overwhelmed or misjudged, creating an emotional chasm that feels difficult to cross. This can lead to frustration and a sense of isolation, as attempts to communicate are not always met with understanding.

Improving clarity and understanding in communication requires deliberate strategies. One valuable method to convey your thoughts and needs effectively is to use simple, direct language. This approach helps minimize ambiguity, making it easier for others to grasp your message without misinterpretation. For instance, instead of saying, "I might need some space," you could state, "I need 10 minutes alone." This clarity can prevent misunderstandings and ensure that your intentions are clear. Visual aids, such as emotion cards, can also assist in expressing feelings. These aids provide a visual representation of emotions, helping bridge the gap between internal experiences and external communication. By showing an emotion card, you can convey complex feelings without needing to find the right words, making interactions smoother and more meaningful.

Establishing healthy boundaries with loved ones is also essential for maintaining respectful and supportive relationships. Boundaries help define personal space, emotional needs, and comfort levels, making it more likely that interactions remain positive and affirming. Articulating boundaries clearly and respectfully helps to establish them. Phrases like "I need some time to myself right now" or "I prefer not to be touched when I'm upset" can communicate your needs without causing offense. Practicing saying "no" politely is also essential, as it empowers you to protect your well-being while maintaining relationships. This type of behavior, which stems from self-knowledge, can take time and practice. Be kind to yourself as you develop this skill. As you learn to express your boundaries consistently, you build a framework for interactions that respects both your needs and those of your loved ones.

Building empathy and understanding within relationships leads to a deeper connection and mutual respect. Engaging in activities that promote empathy can help loved ones appreciate your perspective and experiences. These activities include role-reversal exercises, where family members take on your daily routines, or empathy-building games that encourage open dialogue. Family meetings can also serve as a platform for open communication, allowing everyone to share their thoughts and feelings in a supportive environment. These meetings create a safe space for discussing challenges, celebrating successes, and reinforcing the importance of empathy. By contributing to this culture of understanding, you and your loved ones can navigate communication challenges with compassion and patience, strengthening the bonds that unite you.

Reflection Section: Personal Communication Goals

Take a moment to reflect on your communication experiences with loved ones. Consider the barriers you've encountered and the strategies that have worked well for you. What are your personal communication goals? Write down your thoughts, focusing on areas where you seek improvement and the steps you plan to take. This reflection can guide your journey toward more effective and fulfilling interactions, helping you build stronger connections with those who matter most.

3.2 NAVIGATING SOCIAL INTERACTIONS AT WORK

Navigating the professional environment often feels like stepping into a complex social web where unwritten rules govern interactions. Understanding workplace dynamics is crucial for anyone, but especially for those on the autism spectrum who might find these nuances less instinctual. Office hierarchies dictate how communication flows and decisions are made. Recognizing the structure—who reports to whom, who holds decision-making power—can help you navigate interactions more effectively. It's not just about knowing your manager or team leader; understanding the broader organizational chart can provide a clearer picture of how your role fits into the larger context. Workplaces often have their own particular social norms, which include everything from appropriate dress codes to the expected level of formality in emails. Being aware of these cultural cues can ease your integration into the professional setting and help avoid misunderstandings. Once you are aware of the cues, it becomes a case of balancing your needs with the organization's expectations.

Building interpersonal skills is a fundamental component of thriving in a professional environment. Active listening is one such skill that can significantly enhance your interactions with colleagues. It involves more than just hearing words; it's about understanding the message by paying attention to tone, context, and even body language. Techniques like nodding occasionally, maintaining an appropriate level of eye contact, and paraphrasing to confirm understanding can demonstrate your engagement and respect. Body language awareness is equally important. Nonverbal cues, such as posture and facial expressions, often convey more than words alone. Being mindful of your own and others' body language can help you navigate conversations more smoothly. Participating in team-building activities is another excellent way to develop interpersonal skills. These activities allow you to interact with colleagues in a less formal setting, building rapport and understanding that can translate into more effective collaboration. Whether it's a workshop or a casual team lunch, these opportunities can strengthen your professional relationships.

Conflicts are an inevitable part of any workplace, but how you handle them can define your professional experience. Effective conflict resolution involves a series of steps designed to address issues constructively. First, approach the situation calmly and with an open mind, seeking to understand the other person's perspective. Communicate your thoughts and feelings clearly, focusing on specific behaviors rather than personal attributes. It's essential to listen actively and acknowledge the other person's viewpoint, even if you disagree. Collaboratively brainstorm solutions that address both parties' concerns, aiming for a compromise that benefits everyone. Practicing role-playing conflict scenarios with a trusted colleague or mentor can prepare you for real-life situations. This practice allows you to explore different approaches and refine your conflict resolution skills in a safe environment, building confidence for when such situations arise.

Building a supportive network at work can significantly assist you with growth and development in a professional context. Mentorship programs are an excellent starting point. If your workplace does not offer this feature, you can often find a mentor through other community or mental health resources. Chapter Six explores in depth how to connect with many of these resources. A mentor can offer guidance, share insights, and provide support as you navigate your career. They can also help you understand the unspoken dynamics of the organization, offering advice on how to approach various challenges. Networking events, both formal and informal, are another avenue to expand your professional connections. These events provide a platform to meet colleagues from different departments or organizations, fostering relationships that can lead to new opportunities. Engaging in these networks can open doors to collaborations, professional development, and even potential career advancements. By investing in these relationships, you create a supportive web that enhances your professional journey and provides a sense of belonging within the workplace.

Throughout this exploration of workplace interactions, it's evident that the professional environment is a rich source of complex social cues and dynamics. Understanding these elements can significantly enhance your experience, allowing you to navigate the workplace confidently. Through awareness, skill development, and strategic networking, you can build a fulfilling and supportive professional life.

3.3 BUILDING AND MAINTAINING FRIENDSHIPS

Finding and building friendships can often feel like navigating an uncharted territory. But with a bit of guidance, you can find connections that enrich your life. To begin, identify potential friends by looking for shared interests and activities that excite you. Joining clubs or groups that focus on your passions can provide a natural setting to meet like-minded individuals. Whether it's a book club, a gaming group, or a cooking class, these environments are ripe with opportunities to form connections. Community events, like local fairs or workshops, also offer a chance to meet people outside your usual circles. Being in spaces that align with your interests not only makes interactions more comfortable but also increases the likelihood of meeting people who share your passions. By exploring these activities, you create a fertile ground for friendships to blossom.

Cultivating and sustaining friendships relies on the development of social skills. Engaging in small talk might seem daunting at first, but it can serve as a bridge to deeper conversations. Simple starters like commenting on the weather, asking about someone's weekend plans, or complimenting something you genuinely like can open the door to more meaningful dialogue. Active listening is another helpful skill. It involves focusing entirely on the person speaking, acknowledging their words with nods or brief verbal affirmations, and offering thoughtful responses. Practicing empathy in conversations further enhances these interactions. Try putting yourself in the other person's shoes, considering their feelings and perspectives. By honing these skills, you not only improve your ability to communicate but also show others that you value and respect their contributions to the conversation. These skills lay the groundwork for strong, lasting friendships.

Nurturing and sustaining friendships over time requires effort and intentionality. Regular check-ins are vital to maintaining these bonds. A simple text, call, or message asking how someone is doing can go a long way in showing you care. Planning shared activities is another way to keep the friendship vibrant. Whether it's catching a movie, going for a hike, or trying out a new restaurant, these experiences create shared memories that deepen your connection. It's important to be proactive in suggesting plans and showing interest in spending time together. You don't need to take the initiative all the time; as you do so, it is a cue for the other person to do so, too. Ideally, they will meet you halfway. Consistent communication and shared experiences are the lifeblood of friendships. They keep the relationship dynamic and evolving, allowing you to grow together as friends. This commitment to nurturing the friendship demonstrates your investment in the relationship, encouraging a sense of trust and mutual respect.

Respecting individual differences is crucial in any friendship. Each person brings their own set of experiences, beliefs, and perspectives, which can enrich the relationship if approached with openness. Celebrating diversity within your friend group involves acknowledging and valuing these differences, whether they pertain to culture, background, or personal interests. It means appreciating what each person uniquely contributes to the group. Navigating cultural differences with sensitivity and curiosity can strengthen these bonds. Ask questions, seek to understand, and be willing to learn from one another. This openness to diversity not only broadens your own perspective but also creates an inclusive environment where everyone feels valued. By embracing these differences, you build richer, more resilient friendships that thrive on mutual respect and understanding.

I've seen how these approaches can improve social experiences. My cousin, James, initially found it challenging to engage in small talk. By focusing on his interest in music, he joined a local band group. Here, he met people who shared his passion, making conversations easier and more enjoyable. Over time, James developed the confidence to initiate plans, such as organizing casual jam sessions, which strengthened his connections. His story underscores the power of shared interests in building friendships and the importance of taking the initiative to nurture these relationships. Through persistence and genuine efforts, James found a community where he felt accepted and understood. It highlights that with the right approach, building and maintaining friendships is not only possible but deeply rewarding.

3.4 DATING AND ROMANTIC RELATIONSHIPS

Navigating the world of dating and romantic relationships can be both exhilarating and daunting. Understanding the subtle social cues and dynamics involved in these interactions is crucial. Recognizing signs of interest, for example, is a common area where misinterpretations can occur. You might notice that someone leans in when speaking to you, maintains eye contact, or finds reasons to spend time with you. These are often indicators of interest. However, it's essential to confirm these signals through open communication rather than assumptions to avoid misunderstandings. Understanding consent and boundaries is another vital aspect of these interactions. Consent is about mutual agreement and respect for each other's comfort levels. It's crucial to communicate openly about boundaries, ensuring that you both feel safe and respected. This understanding forms the foundation of any healthy relationship and helps prevent situations where one might feel pressured or uncomfortable.

Online dating has become a popular way to meet potential partners, offering opportunities to connect with people beyond your immediate social circle. However, careful navigation is also required to ensure safety and authenticity. When creating a dating profile, it is important to be honest. Be truthful about your interests, values, and what you're looking for in a relationship. This honesty helps attract individuals who resonate with your true self, setting the stage for genuine connections. Recognizing red flags is also important. Be wary of individuals who avoid answering personal questions, push for personal information too soon, or display inconsistent behavior. These can be signs of someone who may not have your best interests at heart. Maintaining digital privacy is crucial in protecting yourself online. Avoid sharing sensitive information, such as your home address or financial details, with someone you've just met. Use the platform's messaging system until you feel comfortable, and consider meeting in public places for initial encounters. These precautions help ensure your safety while exploring the possibilities of online dating.

Effective communication is the cornerstone of any successful romantic relationship. Expressing your feelings and needs clearly can prevent many common misunderstandings. It involves being honest about your emotions and what you require from the relationship, whether it's more quality time together or respecting your need for personal space. Using 'I' statements, such as "I feel valued when we spend time together," can help convey your message without placing blame. Active listening, especially during disagreements, is equally important. It requires you to focus on understanding your partner's perspective, acknowledging their feelings, and responding thoughtfully. This practice fosters empathy and understanding, which makes conflicts less likely to escalate. Remember, it's not about who wins the argument, but about finding solutions that work for both of you.

Building a healthy romantic relationship involves several key elements, starting with mutual respect and trust. These form the foundation upon which all other aspects are built. Respecting each other's individuality, opinions, and space is important. Trust, on the other hand, is about being reliable and honest, creating a safe space where both partners feel secure. Shared values and goals also play a significant role in the success of a relationship. While differences can enrich a relationship, having common ground in terms of core values and long-term aspirations can strengthen your bond and provide direction. One of the joys and challenges of a relationship is balancing independence and togetherness. While it's wonderful to share experiences and build a life together, maintaining your individuality and engaging in activities separately is equally important. This balance ensures that the relationship remains dynamic and fulfilling, allowing both partners to grow individually and as a couple.

3.5 ASSERTIVE COMMUNICATION: SCRIPTS AND SCENARIOS

Assertive communication is a powerful tool that can help you express yourself clearly and confidently. It involves standing up for your rights while respecting others. Striking this balance leads to mutual respect. Unlike passive communication, which often consists of avoiding confrontation and neglecting your own needs, assertive communication ensures your voice is heard without aggression. Aggressive communication, on the other hand, prioritizes one's own needs over others, often leading to conflicts and damaged relationships. Assertive communication sits comfortably between these extremes, allowing you to articulate your thoughts and needs while considering the perspectives of those around you. Personal interaction in any area is enhanced by this approach. It can also build trust and respect in multiple areas of life.

Creating scripts in advance can be an effective way to prepare for situations that require assertiveness. These scripts serve as templates to guide your responses, which help to maintain clarity and confidence. For instance, when requesting accommodations at work, you might say, "I perform best in a quiet environment. Could we discuss options for minimizing noise around my workspace?" This script clearly states your need and opens the door for discussion without confrontation. Declining social invitations can be tricky, but assertiveness can help you maintain your boundaries. You might say, "Thank you for inviting me, but I need some time to recharge. Let's catch up another time." This response respects both your needs and the invitation, preserving the relationship while respecting your boundaries. By preparing these scripts in advance, you can navigate challenging situations with poise and assurance.

Practicing assertive communication through role-playing exercises is another way to build confidence and reduce anxiety around communication. Engaging in feedback scenarios with coworkers can provide a safe space to rehearse and refine your approach. For example, you could practice giving constructive feedback by role-playing with a friend or coach, focusing on using "I" statements and maintaining a calm tone. This exercise helps you articulate your thoughts clearly and respectfully, ensuring your message is received well. Family discussions about personal needs can also benefit from role-playing. Practicing these conversations allows you to explore different strategies and responses, building confidence for real-life situations. If you do not have anyone with whom to role-play, even speaking out loud to yourself helps integrate these techniques into your social repertoire. These exercises not only enhance your communication skills but also reduce anxiety by familiarizing you with potential scenarios and responses.

Overcoming communication anxiety helps significantly in maintaining assertiveness in interactions. One effective technique is practicing breathing exercises before conversations. Deep, slow breaths can calm your nervous system, reducing anxiety and preparing you to speak clearly. Visualizing a positive outcome can also help alleviate stress, allowing you to approach the conversation with a more relaxed mindset. Positive self-affirmations are another powerful tool. Remind yourself of your strengths and abilities, reinforcing your confidence and self-worth. Phrases like "I have the right to express my needs" or "I am capable of handling this situation" can shift your mindset, empowering you to communicate assertively. Combining these techniques can create a strong foundation for assertive communication, allowing you to handle your communications with more confidence and success.

As you develop these assertive communication skills, remember that practice and patience are key. It might take time to feel comfortable using these techniques, but each step forward strengthens your ability to express yourself effectively. By integrating assertiveness into your daily interactions, you can build relationships grounded in respect and understanding, which can, in turn, enrich your personal and professional life. In the next chapter, we will explore tools and strategies for enhancing executive functioning, offering practical solutions to improve daily organization and task management.

FOUR

NAVIGATING PROFESSIONAL LIFE

I magine stepping into a new workplace. The walls are adorned with vibrant posters, and the hum of conversation fills the air. Yet, as you enter, you notice something different. The air is calm, the lights are soft, and there are quiet nooks where employees can retreat. This is no ordinary office; it's an environment crafted with neurodiversity in mind. Such spaces are no longer rare. Companies are increasingly recognizing the value of inclusive workplaces that cater to the diverse needs of their employees. Navigating professional life as an adult with autism can be daunting, but finding an autism-friendly workplace can make all the difference. This chapter will guide you through identifying and evaluating potential employers, advocating for your needs, managing challenges, and thriving in non-traditional roles.

4.1 ASSESSING POTENTIAL WORKPLACES

Recognizing inclusive companies begins with understanding the indicators of a supportive company culture. Look for explicit statements about diversity and inclusion in the company's mission or values. These declarations often reflect a genuine commitment to fostering an inclusive environment. Companies that support neurodiversity typically have diversity and inclusion policies in place, outlining their efforts to accommodate diverse needs. Employee testimonials can also provide valuable insights. Current and former employees often share their experiences on platforms like Glassdoor, where you can gauge how well a company supports its neurodiverse staff. Positive testimonials can highlight the availability of accommodations, an understanding of management, or a culture that values diverse perspectives. These indicators collectively paint a picture of a company's commitment to inclusivity, allowing you to assess whether it aligns with your needs and values.

To research specific potential employers, delve deeper into their practices and policies. Start by examining company websites and social media channels for diversity initiatives. Many organizations proudly showcase their efforts to create inclusive environments, detailing programs designed to support neurodiverse employees. This information can provide a clear indication of the company's priorities and its approach to diversity. When researching, pay attention to how the company addresses neurodiversity specifically, as this can be a strong indicator of their readiness to accommodate and support autistic employees. By gathering this information, you can make informed decisions about potential workplaces.

An interview can be a valuable time to determine if a workplace will be a good fit for your needs. During interviews, take the opportunity to ask questions about workplace accommodations. Inquire about the company's policies on adjusting workspaces, flexible hours, or other support measures. You might ask, "Can you tell me about your diversity and inclusion initiatives, specifically regarding neurodiversity?" Observing the office layout and dynamics during visits can also provide valuable insights. Look for signs of an inclusive environment, such as quiet areas for breaks or adjustable lighting. These features can indicate the company's commitment to accommodating diverse needs. If you can, notice how employees interact with one another. A respectful and open atmosphere often reflects a positive company culture. By assessing these elements during your interview, you can better determine if the workplace is conducive to your comfort and success.

Networking with current employees offers another layer of insight into a company's culture and inclusivity. Use LinkedIn to identify mutual connections who can provide an insider's perspective on the workplace. Reaching out to these contacts can yield valuable information about the company's day-to-day operations and the experiences of its neurodiverse employees. Participating in informational interviews can also be helpful. These informal conversations allow you to gather first-hand accounts of what it's like to work at the company. Ask questions about the company's approach to accommodations, the general work environment, and any challenges related to neurodiversity. Current employees can provide honest feedback, helping you assess whether the company aligns with your needs and values. Building these connections not only aids in your job search but also expands your professional network, offering support and insights throughout your career journey.

Reflection Section: Assessing Workplace Culture

Take a moment to reflect on what you value most in a workplace. Consider aspects like company culture, accommodations, and diversity initiatives. How do these elements align with your personal and professional goals? Make a list of questions to ask during interviews that will help you evaluate these aspects. This reflection will guide you in finding a workplace that genuinely supports your well-being and growth.

4.2 SELF-ADVOCACY IN EMPLOYMENT

Understanding your rights as an autistic employee is crucial in navigating the workplace confidently. In the USA, the Americans with Disabilities Act (ADA) delineates and enshrines your rights, offering protection against discrimination and ensuring access to reasonable accommodations. As defined by the ADA, reasonable accommodations are modifications or adjustments to a job or work environment that enable a person with a disability to perform essential job functions. This means that as an autistic employee, you have the right to request changes that will support your ability to work effectively. Standard accommodations might include adjustments like flexible scheduling, quiet workspaces, or specialized equipment. The ADA requires employers with 15 or more employees to provide these accommodations unless doing so would cause undue hardship. Understanding these rights empowers you to advocate for the support you need, creating a more accessible and inclusive work environment. If you are not located in the USA, it is well worth researching any similar organizations in your region that will support you.

Your workplace experience can be significantly enhanced by your ability to communicate your needs effectively. Start by drafting a clear accommodation request letter. This document should outline the specific accommodations you need and how they will assist you in fulfilling your job responsibilities. Be concise and focus on the connection between the accommodation and your job performance. Timing is crucial when approaching your supervisor with these requests. Choose a moment when they are likely to be receptive and have the time to discuss your needs in depth. Approach the conversation with a collaborative mindset, emphasizing your commitment to performing your job well with the proper support. Successful accommodation requests often include examples, such as, "I find that a quieter workspace would help me focus and reduce sensory overload, thereby improving my productivity." This approach not only clarifies your needs but also demonstrates how the accommodation benefits both you and the organization.

Building confidence in self-advocacy is an ongoing process. The assertive communication skills you started developing in the prior chapter are highly valuable in workplace environments as well. Assertiveness allows you to express your needs clearly and respectfully without being passive or aggressive. It involves using "I" statements to convey your perspective, such as "I need a few minutes to process information before responding." Role-playing advocacy scenarios with a trusted friend or mentor can effectively develop these skills, as can practicing in a mirror. Through role-play, you can simulate conversations with your employer, experimenting with different approaches and receiving feedback. This practice builds your confidence, enabling you to navigate real-world interactions with greater ease. As you become more comfortable asserting your needs, you'll find it easier to advocate for yourself effectively, ensuring that your workplace supports your success.

In the event of employer pushback, a resilient and strategic response can be helpful. If your accommodation request is denied, it's important to understand the reason behind the decision. Ask for clarification and explore alternative solutions that address both your needs and the employer's concerns. Engaging in a constructive dialogue can often lead to a compromise that benefits both parties. If the situation remains unresolved, consider seeking support from your Human Resources (HR) department or external advocacy groups. HR can mediate the conversation and help facilitate a resolution. Advocacy organizations, such as the Job Accommodation Network, can provide guidance and resources to support your case. Remember that the ADA is on your side, and organizations are legally obligated to engage in an interactive process to find adequate accommodations. By leveraging these resources, you can navigate pushback with confidence, ensuring that your rights are respected and upheld.

In all these aspects of self-advocacy, remember that you are not alone. Many others have walked this path, and there are communities and resources available to support you. Embrace your rights and the power of your voice, knowing that advocating for yourself is a crucial step in creating a fulfilling and supportive professional life.

4.3 MANAGING EXECUTIVE DYSFUNCTION AT WORK

Executive dysfunction can be a significant hurdle in the workplace, yet understanding it is the first step toward managing it effectively. At its core, executive dysfunction refers to difficulties in cognitive processes that help with organizing, planning, and executing tasks. You might find yourself struggling to initiate tasks, keep track of time, or manage priorities, which can lead to challenges in meeting deadlines or maintaining productivity. Common symptoms include forgetfulness, trouble with task-switching, and an overwhelming feeling when faced with complex projects. These challenges can manifest in various ways, such as missing meetings due to poor time management or feeling paralyzed by the need to start a big task. Recognizing these patterns is the first step, as it allows you to identify specific areas where support and strategies can make a significant difference.

A number of different tools can assist with improving task management. Explore whether you respond more to visual cues or auditory ones. One effective tool is using task management apps, which can help you organize tasks, set reminders, and track progress. Apps like Todoist or Trello offer visual layouts that can simplify complex projects into manageable steps. Another visual technique is to map out your day, whether on a whiteboard or color-coded in a planner. You can allocate time for specific tasks, ensuring that you stay on track and avoid the pitfalls of procrastination. Implementing the Pomodoro Technique can also enhance your focus and efficiency. This method involves working in short bursts, typically 25 minutes, followed by a short break. It helps maintain concentration and reduces the anxiety of long, uninterrupted work sessions. You could use a timer that is purely auditory, vibrates on an accessory you are wearing, or both. These tools collectively support your ability to manage tasks effectively, reducing the stress associated with executive dysfunction.

When exploring tools and techniques, it is important to work with your individual preferences. When I first became self-employed, I struggled greatly with time management. I explored a variety of online and physical tools. Through trial and error, I discovered that a combination of an electronic calendar and a physical notebook works best for me. I needed more than one or the other to engage me. The notebook needs to be of a specific size and paper type, which I use with a writing implement whose color and pen feel I particularly like. Integrate your unique preferences into a system that works best for you. It can even be enjoyable!

Creating a conducive environment can enhance focus and productivity in the workplace. Setting up a distraction-free workspace is a good place to start. Consider arranging your desk to minimize clutter and using noise-canceling headphones to block out disruptive sounds. This setup can help you maintain concentration and create a mental boundary between work and distractions. Time-blocking for deep work is another powerful technique. By scheduling dedicated blocks of time for focused work, you can tackle complex tasks with greater efficiency. During these periods, turn off notifications and commit to uninterrupted work. This practice not only boosts productivity but also reduces the cognitive load associated with task-switching. Establishing these habits can transform your work environment into a space that engenders focus and achievement.

Seeking support and accommodations is an essential aspect of managing executive dysfunction in the workplace. Requesting flexible deadlines can provide the breathing room needed to execute tasks without the pressure of tight time constraints. This flexibility allows you to work at a pace that aligns with your cognitive rhythm, enhancing the quality of your output. Utilizing job coaching services can also offer personalized support. A job coach can help you develop strategies tailored to your strengths and challenges, offering guidance on organizing tasks and improving time management. These services provide an external perspective and accountability, helping you stay on track. Open communication with your employer about your needs is crucial for accessing these supports. By advocating for yourself and leveraging available resources, you can create a work environment that accommodates your unique needs and maximizes your potential.

4.4 THRIVING IN NON-TRADITIONAL WORK ENVIRONMENTS

The landscape of work is evolving, offering new opportunities for those who thrive outside traditional office settings. Flexible work arrangements, such as remote work and freelance opportunities, have opened doors for many, especially for autistic adults. Remote work provides a unique chance to craft an environment tailored to your sensory needs. You can control lighting, noise, and even your schedule, creating a space where you feel most productive. This adaptability can significantly reduce stress and enhance focus, allowing you to work at your best. Additionally, freelance and contract work offer a level of autonomy that traditional roles might not. Here, you can choose projects that align with your interests and strengths, creating a career path that feels both fulfilling and manageable.

Balancing structure and flexibility in these non-traditional roles is essential. You will need to develop a personalized work routine to help maintain productivity while accommodating your unique needs. Start by setting specific work hours that suit your natural rhythm, allowing for periods of intense focus and necessary breaks. This structure provides consistency while giving you the flexibility to adjust as needed. Setting boundaries is equally important, especially in roles that blend work and personal life. Clearly define your work hours and communicate them to clients or colleagues. This delineation ensures that work does not encroach on personal time, promoting a healthy work-life balance. By establishing these boundaries, you create a framework that supports both your professional ambitions and personal well-being.

In non-traditional work environments, your traits can become powerful assets. Creative problem-solving abilities often shine in freelance projects, where innovative solutions are prized. These roles frequently require thinking outside the box, an area where many autistic individuals excel. Your attention to detail can also be a significant advantage. In projects that demand precision, such as editing, design, or data analysis, this trait ensures high-quality outcomes. Embrace these strengths and seek opportunities that allow them to flourish. Recognizing how your unique attributes contribute to success in these settings can boost your confidence and satisfaction. It transforms perceived challenges into strengths, allowing you to approach work with a sense of empowerment.

Finding community in non-traditional work settings might seem daunting, but it's entirely possible. Engaging with online free-lancer communities can provide a sense of connection and support. Platforms like Upwork or Freelancer offer forums and groups where you can share experiences, seek advice, and collabo-rate with others. These communities create a sense of belonging, reminding you that you're not navigating this path alone. Additionally, attending co-working space events can offer both networking opportunities and a break from the isolation of remote work. Many cities have spaces where freelancers gather, providing a blend of social interaction and professional develop-ment. These events can introduce you to potential collaborators or clients, expanding your professional network. By building connec-tions in these ways, you create a support system that enriches both your personal and professional life.

4.5 NEURODIVERSE NETWORKING AND CAREER GROWTH

Building a professional network is a vital step in advancing your career. It opens doors to opportunities, provides support, and encourages connections that can lead to personal and professional growth. Attending conferences, if they exist in your industry, is an excellent way to start. These gatherings bring together profes-sionals from various fields, offering a platform to learn about the latest trends and innovations. They also provide a unique oppor-tunity to meet potential collaborators and mentors. As you engage with others, focus on shared interests and experiences, which can serve as a foundation for lasting connections. Similarly, joining professional groups and associations can expand your network. These organizations often host events, workshops, and forums that encourage interaction among members. By participating actively, you can build relationships with peers who share your professional goals. These connections often lead to collaborations, job opportunities, and valuable insights that can enhance your career. Your newfound assertive communication skills will serve you well here, as in other areas.

Utilizing networking tools effectively can further enhance your ability to connect with others. LinkedIn is one such platform for building and maintaining professional relationships. Start by optimizing your profile to reflect your skills, experiences, and career aspirations. A well-crafted profile can attract potential employers and collaborators, showcasing your unique strengths and contributions. Engage in online forums and discussion groups that align with your interests. These virtual spaces offer a wealth of knowledge and perspectives, allowing you to exchange ideas and advice with like-minded individuals. By contributing to discussions and sharing your insights, you can establish yourself as a knowledgeable and engaged member of the community. This visibility can lead to new connections and opportunities, broadening your network and strengthening your professional presence.

Mentorship plays a crucial role in career development, offering guidance, support, and insight from experienced professionals. Finding mentors within your industry can provide you with valuable perspectives on navigating your career path. Mentors can share their experiences, offer advice on overcoming challenges, and help you identify opportunities for growth. Participating in mentorship programs is one way to connect with mentors. Many organizations offer structured programs that pair mentees with seasoned professionals. These programs provide a framework for building meaningful relationships, ensuring that you receive the support and guidance you need to succeed. Through mentorship, you can gain confidence, develop new skills, and make informed decisions about your career trajectory.

Advancing through continued learning is essential for career growth, especially in today's rapidly evolving job market. Enrolling in online courses can help you acquire new skills and knowledge relevant to your field. Many platforms offer a wide range of courses, covering everything from technical skills to leadership and communication. By staying current with industry trends and expanding your skill set, you position yourself as a valuable asset to employers. Attending workshops and seminars is another way to enhance your expertise. These events provide hands-on learning experiences and opportunities to interact with experts and peers. They can also spark new ideas and inspire creativity, fueling your passion for your work. Pursuing certifications relevant to your career goals can further bolster your credentials. Certifications demonstrate your commitment to professional development and can enhance your credibility in the eyes of employers. By investing in your education, you equip yourself with the tools needed to excel in your career.

As you navigate the landscape of professional growth, remember that building a network, seeking mentorship, and continuing your education are interconnected endeavors. They provide a foundation for success, empowering you to pursue your ambitions with confidence and resilience. Each connection and learning opportunity contributes to your development, helping you build a fulfilling and rewarding career. With these strategies in mind, you can navigate your professional life with purpose and clarity, embracing the opportunities that come your way.

FIVE
SELF-CARE AND MENTAL HEALTH

Picture yourself standing at a shoreline, watching the waves gently roll in and out, a natural rhythm that soothes and calms. Mindfulness can create a similar sense of balance in your mind, offering a moment of peace amid life's chaos. This chapter explores mindfulness techniques tailored for autistic adults, focusing on how these practices can reduce stress and enhance your overall well-being. Mindfulness, at its core, is the practice of being fully present in the moment and aware of your thoughts, feelings, and surroundings without judgment. It is a tool that can help you manage the stressors of daily life and foster a deeper connection with yourself and the world around you.

5.1 BENEFITS OF MINDFULNESS

Understanding mindfulness begins with recognizing its benefits, particularly for those on the autism spectrum. The practice of mindfulness can serve as a powerful stress-reduction tool, providing a respite from the constant flood of sensory input and the pressures of social interactions. By focusing your attention on the present moment, you can create a mental space that allows you to process experiences calmly and deliberately. This can reduce feelings of overwhelm and anxiety, promoting a sense of inner peace. Mindfulness also enhances focus and awareness, helping you engage more fully with tasks and interactions. By cultivating this heightened awareness, you can improve your ability to concentrate and respond thoughtfully rather than react impulsively.

Many traditional mindfulness practices are already sensory-friendly, but if necessary, they can be further adapted to suit autistic needs. For example, you could create a quiet, comfortable space with minimal sensory distractions for your meditation. Soft lighting, gentle sounds, or even the soothing presence of a weighted blanket can enhance this environment. Short, focused breathing exercises are another adaptable mindfulness technique. These exercises involve taking slow, deep breaths and focusing your attention on the sensation of each breath entering and leaving your body. This practice can be particularly beneficial in moments of stress or agitation, providing a quick and accessible way to regain composure and clarity.

Incorporating mindfulness into everyday activities can transform routine tasks into opportunities for reflection and growth without the need to carve out specific time for such practices. Mindful eating is one such practice, where you focus on the sensory experience of your meals—observing the colors, textures, and flavors of each bite. This approach not only enhances your enjoyment of food but also encourages a more intentional relationship with nourishment. Engaging in mindful walks is another way to integrate mindfulness into your daily life. As you walk, pay attention to the sensation of your feet touching the ground, the rhythm of your steps, and the sights and sounds around you. These walks can become a form of moving meditation, offering a chance to connect with nature and yourself in a deliberate and meaningful way.

Technology can be a valuable ally in supporting your mindfulness journey. Guided meditation apps offer a structured yet flexible way to practice mindfulness, providing you with audio or visual cues to guide your focus and awareness. These apps often include a variety of meditation styles and durations, allowing you to choose what resonates with you. Virtual reality mindfulness experiences are a newer innovation, offering immersive environments designed to enhance relaxation and presence. These experiences can transport you to serene landscapes or calming spaces, providing an engaging way to practice mindfulness. By using technology in this way, you can tailor your mindfulness practice to fit your preferences and needs, making it a more accessible and enjoyable part of your routine.

Reflection Section: Exploring Mindfulness Tools

Explore different mindfulness tools and techniques to find what works best for you. Try a guided meditation app and note how it affects your mood and focus. Experiment with mindful eating and observe how it changes your perception of meals. Reflect on these experiences in a journal, noting any shifts in your stress levels or awareness. This reflection can help you identify the practices that resonate most deeply, allowing you to build a mindfulness routine that supports your well-being and enriches your life.

5.2 COPING WITH ANXIETY AND DEPRESSION

Recognizing the symptoms of anxiety and depression in autistic adults is essential for managing these conditions effectively. Emotionally, you might experience intense feelings of worry or fear that persistently linger, affecting your mood and outlook. Physically, anxiety can manifest as headaches, stomachaches, or a racing heart. These symptoms often compound, leading to behavioral changes such as withdrawal from social interactions or a noticeable decline in activities you usually enjoy. Depression, on the other hand, may present as enduring sadness or a lack of interest in life. You might feel fatigued, have trouble concentrating, or experience changes in sleep and appetite. Recognizing these signs early can be the first step towards seeking help and finding relief.

Developing coping strategies to manage anxiety and depression can empower you to take control of your mental health. Creating environments that reduce anxiety can be immensely beneficial. Consider arranging your living space to minimize clutter and noise, creating a calm and organized atmosphere that promotes relaxation. Cognitive-behavioral techniques (CBT) offer another avenue for managing these challenges. These techniques involve identifying and challenging negative thought patterns and replacing them with more balanced and realistic ones. For instance, if you find yourself thinking, "I can't handle this," try reframing it to, "This is challenging, but I can manage it with support." This shift in perspective can reduce the hold of anxiety and depression, allowing you to respond more adaptively to stressors. If you would like to explore this method in more detail, there are CBT books and workbooks to assist you in going deeper.

Building a strong support network is very helpful for coping with anxiety and depression. It need not be large. A small network is fine if the connections are authentic. Connecting with family and friends who understand your experiences can provide comfort and encouragement. Share your feelings with those you trust, and let them know how they can support you. Sometimes, having someone simply listen can be incredibly validating. Joining mental health support groups can also help. These groups offer a community of individuals who share similar experiences, providing a sense of belonging and understanding. Participating in group discussions can offer new perspectives and coping strategies, reminding you that you are not alone in your struggles. A strong support network can be a source of strength and resilience, helping you navigate difficult times with greater ease.

There are times when seeking professional help becomes necessary. Recognizing the signs that indicate the need for therapy is crucial. If you find that anxiety or depression is significantly impacting your daily life, such as affecting your ability to work or maintain relationships, it may be time to reach out to a mental health professional. Types of professionals include psychologists, who offer therapy and counseling, and psychiatrists, who can prescribe medications if needed. It is essential to find a therapist who is informed about autism, as they will better understand your unique experiences and tailor their approach accordingly. An autism-informed therapist can provide strategies that respect your sensory and communication needs, making therapy more effective and comfortable for you. Seeking professional help is a proactive step towards improving your mental health and reclaiming your well-being.

Recognizing symptoms, developing coping strategies, building a support system, and knowing when to seek professional help are all important steps in managing anxiety and depression. By understanding these elements, you can create a comprehensive approach to mental health that supports your unique needs and develops resilience. Remember, managing anxiety and depression is not about eliminating these feelings entirely but instead learning to manage them with confidence and support. Through these efforts, you can cultivate a life that prioritizes well-being and empowerment, allowing you to thrive amidst the challenges you face.

5.3 ESTABLISHING A PERSONALIZED SELF-CARE ROUTINE

Self-care is a crucial concept for everyone, but especially for autistic adults. It signifies the intentional actions you take to maintain and improve your mental well-being. In the context of autism, self-care becomes even more significant as it helps manage the unique stressors you may face daily. It is not just about occasional pampering or indulgence; it's about forming habits that support your mental and emotional health consistently. The individualized approach to self-care means recognizing that what works for one person might not work for another. Your self-care needs are personal, shaped by your preferences, sensory sensitivities, and daily challenges. Understanding this allows you to create a self-care routine that truly benefits you, helping you traverse life with greater ease and resilience.

Identifying personal needs and preferences is the first step in crafting an effective self-care routine. Start by keeping a self-care journal where you can jot down activities that make you feel relaxed or rejuvenated. This journal serves as a repository for your thoughts and observations, helping you identify patterns in what uplifts your spirit and what drains it. Experimentation is key. Try different activities, such as taking a quiet walk in nature, enjoying a warm bath, or engaging in a favorite hobby. Then, note how each makes you feel. Over time, this process will reveal which activities resonate most with you, helping you tailor your self-care routine to your unique needs. By understanding what truly nourishes you, you can focus your efforts on self-care practices that have the most impact.

Creating a self-care plan involves more than just listing activities; it requires structuring them into your life in a sustainable way. Begin by scheduling regular self-care time, treating it with the same importance as any other commitment. This might mean setting aside a few minutes each morning for reflection or dedicating a weekend afternoon to relaxation. Consistency is crucial, as regular self-care can prevent burnout and maintain your well-being over time. Incorporate a variety of activities into your routine to address different needs. Physical activities like stretching or a brief exercise session can boost your mood, while quieter pursuits like reading or listening to music can provide mental rest. A balanced self-care plan ensures that you're nurturing every aspect of your well-being, offering a holistic approach to self-care.

Despite the benefits, maintaining a self-care routine can present challenges. Time management is a common obstacle, particularly when juggling multiple responsibilities. It's easy to let self-care fall by the wayside when life gets busy. To counter this, prioritize self-care by viewing it as an essential part of your life rather than an optional extra. Utilize tools like planners or digital reminders to allocate specific times for self-care, to make sure it becomes a regular part of your schedule. Another barrier might be the feeling of guilt or selfishness when taking time for yourself. Remember that self-care is not selfish; it's necessary for maintaining your health and well-being. Involving accountability partners can help you stay committed to your self-care routine. Share your goals with a friend or family member who supports your well-being, or identify a friend or loved one who wishes to prioritize their own self-care. They can offer encouragement and remind you to prioritize yourself, even when it feels challenging.

The pursuit of self-care is deeply personal and requires a thoughtful understanding of your needs. By defining what self-care means to you and identifying activities that support your well-being, you create a foundation for a sustainable routine. Structuring this routine into your life, overcoming obstacles, and involving supportive individuals can help you maintain these practices over time. Self-care is about honoring yourself and your needs, providing the space to recharge and thrive in a world that can sometimes feel overwhelming. As you develop and refine your self-care plan, remember that the goal is to support your mental and emotional health, empowering you to engage with life with resilience and confidence. By embracing this individualized approach, you can build a self-care routine that enriches your life and enhances your well-being.

5.4 CREATIVE OUTLETS FOR STRESS RELIEF

Artistic expression offers a sanctuary for the mind, a place where stress can transform into creativity and healing. For autistic adults, this form of expression can be particularly potent. Engaging in creative activities allows you to channel emotions constructively, providing a non-verbal outlet for feelings that might otherwise remain unexpressed. Whether it's the brushstrokes of a painting capturing the hues of your mood or the rhythm of words flowing across a page, creativity can serve as a therapeutic release. This process not only alleviates stress but also facilitates personal growth, enabling you to explore and understand your emotions in a safe and supportive way. Through art, you can find a voice for your inner world, communicating complex feelings that might be difficult to articulate otherwise.

Exploring different creative mediums can open new avenues for self-discovery and stress relief. Painting and drawing offer visual expression, allowing you to create images that reflect your thoughts and emotions. The act of translating feelings into colors and shapes can be meditative, providing clarity and focus. Writing, too, serves as a form of self-reflection, where you can weave narratives or poetry that capture your experiences. This form of expression can be particularly cathartic, as it offers a structured way to process and organize your thoughts. Music, with its capacity to evoke emotion and memory, can also be a calming influence. Whether you're playing an instrument, singing, or simply listening, music can soothe the mind and body, offering a sense of peace and connection. Each medium presents unique opportunities to engage with your inner self, allowing for a personalized approach to creativity and stress relief.

Incorporating creativity into your daily life can enhance your well-being significantly. Consider setting up a dedicated creative space in your home, a corner where you can immerse yourself in artistic pursuits without distraction. This space need not be elaborate; even a simple desk with your favorite supplies can become a haven for creativity. Allocate specific times for creative activities, making them a regular part of your routine. These sessions could be as brief as fifteen minutes or span a leisurely afternoon, depending on your schedule and needs. The key is consistency, ensuring that creativity remains an integral part of your life. By making time for art, you create a rhythm that supports self-expression and relaxation, nurturing your mental health and resilience.

Creative pursuits can be individual activities, or they can involve community and collaborative elements. Joining local art groups or taking a class can provide a supportive environment where you can share your work and learn from others. These groups often host workshops, exhibitions, and gatherings that encourage collaboration and feedback. Participating in these activities can deepen your understanding of your craft while providing a sense of belonging. Online creative challenges are another avenue to explore. These challenges, often hosted on social media or dedicated platforms, invite participants to create within specific themes or prompts. Engaging in these challenges can spark inspiration, pushing you to experiment and grow. The sense of community and shared purpose can be motivating, reminding you that creativity can be a collective experience as much as a personal one.

Interactive Element: Creative Expression Journal

Starting a creative expression journal can be a revealing way to document your artistic journey. Use this space to record your thoughts, sketches, and ideas. Reflect on how each creative session affects your mood and stress levels. Note any patterns or themes that emerge in your work. This journal can be a valuable tool for personal growth, offering insights into your creative process and emotional landscape. Over time, it can become a cherished record of your artistic exploration and self-discovery, a testament to the power of creativity in your life.

5.5 NAVIGATING HEALTHCARE AS AN AUTISTIC ADULT

Navigating the healthcare system can often feel daunting, especially for autistic adults who may face unique challenges in these settings. It's important to know your rights as a patient within the healthcare system, which can empower you to advocate for your needs effectively. Patient rights include the right to respectful care, privacy, and the ability to make informed decisions about your treatment. Informed consent is a critical aspect of this, ensuring that you have all the necessary information to make educated choices about your healthcare. This means that healthcare providers must explain treatment options and risks in a way that you can understand, allowing you to consent or refuse based on a clear understanding of what is involved. Being aware of these rights ensures that you are an active participant in your healthcare rather than a passive recipient.

Preparing for healthcare appointments can significantly enhance your experience and the quality of care you receive. One effective strategy is to create a list of questions and concerns before your appointment. This ensures that you address all the issues important to you without forgetting anything in the moment. Consider listing symptoms, medications, or any changes in your condition that you wish to discuss. Bringing a support person can also be beneficial. This person can provide emotional support, help remember details, and assist in communication if needed. Having someone with you can alleviate anxiety and ensure that your concerns are effectively communicated. Additionally, using communication aids, such as written notes or visual aids, can help convey your needs and preferences clearly. These tools can be particularly useful in environments where verbal communication might be challenging. Preparing thoroughly can increase the likelihood of a productive and less stressful healthcare experience.

Finding autism-friendly healthcare providers can make a significant difference in the quality of care you receive. Start by researching providers' backgrounds to determine their experience and understanding of autism. Look for those who have specific training or experience working with autistic individuals, as they are more likely to be sensitive to your needs. Seeking recommendations from the autistic community can also be invaluable. Online forums, support groups, or local autism organizations can provide insights into which providers are most accommodating and understanding. These recommendations guide you to professionals who are more likely to provide compassionate and informed care. Choosing the right healthcare provider is a step towards ensuring that your healthcare experiences are supportive and respectful of your needs.

Healthcare anxiety is a common challenge, but there are techniques that can help manage this stress. Visualization exercises can help reduce anxiety before appointments. Try envisioning the appointment going smoothly, focusing on calming images or scenarios that relax you. This practice can help reduce anticipatory anxiety, setting a more positive tone for the actual visit. Familiarizing yourself with medical environments can also alleviate anxiety. Visit the clinic or office beforehand to become accustomed to the setting. Knowing what to expect can reduce sensory overload and provide a sense of control. If a pre-visit isn't possible, ask the office staff to describe the environment and what you might encounter. This knowledge can ease the transition into the appointment, making the experience more manageable. These strategies empower you to approach healthcare settings with greater confidence and calmness.

Navigating healthcare as an autistic adult involves understanding your rights, preparing for appointments, finding accommodating providers, and managing anxiety. By equipping yourself with these strategies, you can take an active role in your healthcare, ensuring that your needs are met with respect and understanding. These efforts contribute to a more positive and empowering healthcare experience, allowing you to prioritize your well-being while maintaining your autonomy. As we conclude this chapter, consider how these practices can integrate with your broader self-care strategy, fostering a holistic approach to health that supports your unique needs. In the next chapter, we will explore community and support networks, focusing on how these connections can enhance your life and well-being.

MAKE A DIFFERENCE WITH YOUR REVIEW
UNLOCK THE POWER OF GENEROSITY

"Every person, no matter what their wealth, is equally capable of practicing generosity."

THICH NHAT HANH

People who give without expecting anything in return often lead happier, more fulfilling lives. By sharing your experience with **Living with Adult Autism: Practical Tools for Executive Functioning, Sensory Overload, and Better Communication, so You Can Thrive Unmasked**, you have the chance to make a difference for someone navigating the same challenges you've faced.

My mission is to support autistic adults and those who care about them. But to reach more people, I need your help.

Most readers rely on reviews to decide whether a book is right for them. By leaving a review, you can be the voice that encourages someone else to begin their journey toward better understanding and self-acceptance.

It costs nothing, and takes less than five minutes. Thank you for leaving a review on the platform where you purchased this book.

Warmly,
Claude Moore

SIX

BUILDING COMMUNITY AND SUPPORT NETWORKS

E nvision yourself in a room filled with people who understand you without the need for explanation. This room exists in the digital realm, where the walls are virtual, and the connections are real. Finding a community that resonates with your experiences as an autistic adult can be transformative. In this chapter, we will explore how to find and engage with online communities, offering a sense of belonging and support. The online world provides unique opportunities to connect with others who share your journey.

6.1 FINDING YOUR AUTISM COMMUNITY ONLINE

The digital landscape is vast, offering numerous platforms where autistic individuals can find community and support. Social media groups dedicated to autism are a good starting point. These groups provide spaces for sharing experiences, seeking advice, and celebrating milestones with others who understand your perspective. Platforms like Facebook host numerous autism-focused groups where members discuss topics ranging from daily challenges to advocacy efforts. Each group has its own culture and rules, so exploring several can help you find the best fit. Like all online and social media groups, they are not perfect: take the time to explore them to judge their quality and appropriateness.

Autism-focused forums and discussion boards offer another avenue for connection. Websites such as Reddit host forums where you can engage in conversations about specific interests or concerns. These platforms often provide a more structured environment than social media, with threads dedicated to particular topics. This structure can be helpful if you prefer organized discussions or have specific questions in mind. Additionally, forums can be a rich source of information, with members sharing resources and insights that can enrich your understanding of how autism manifests in your life.

For those who prefer real-time communication, Discord servers can be an excellent resource. Discord is a platform that hosts servers—essentially chat rooms—where members can converse through text, voice, or video. Many autism-focused Discord servers offer channels dedicated to various topics, from socializing and gaming to mental health support. This format allows for immediate interaction, creating a sense of presence and community even when miles apart. Being part of a Discord server can feel like joining a virtual club where everyone shares a common interest in autism.

When considering joining an online community, it's vital to evaluate its quality and safety. Look for communities with clear moderation policies and community guidelines. These elements help ensure a respectful and supportive environment. Moderators play an essential role in maintaining the tone of the group, addressing conflicts, and ensuring rules are followed. A community's diversity and inclusivity are also important factors. A diverse membership can provide a wealth of perspectives and foster an environment where everyone feels valued. Inclusivity ensures that voices from all backgrounds and experiences are heard, enriching the community as a whole.

Participating in online discussions requires a thoughtful approach to communication. Respectful communication etiquette is key to positive interactions. This means being mindful of your language, respecting differing opinions, and avoiding inflammatory comments. Sharing personal experiences and insights can be a powerful way to connect with others. It allows you to offer support and understanding while also gaining new perspectives. Remember that everyone in an online community brings their own experiences and challenges. Approaching conversations with empathy and an open mind can lead to meaningful connections and create a supportive network.

Building virtual friendships offers both benefits and challenges. The ability to connect with people worldwide is a significant advantage. Virtual meetups and events allow you to participate in activities and discussions without the constraints of geography. These interactions can lead to genuine friendships where support and camaraderie flourish. However, online relationships also require effort and patience. Unlike face-to-face interactions, virtual friendships may take longer to develop. Trust and under-standing build gradually as you engage in conversations and participate in community events. They are also not a substitute for in-person, face-to-face relationships. However, they can provide an additional layer of support.

Collaborative online projects can further deepen these connec-tions. Working together on shared interests or goals can create a sense of purpose and unity. Whether it's joining a virtual book club, participating in a writing challenge, or contributing to an advocacy effort, these projects can manifest teamwork and creativity. They provide an opportunity to share your strengths and learn from others, enhancing both personal growth and community cohesion.

Reflection Section: Evaluating an Online Community

Take some time to explore an online community that interests you. Observe the interactions and consider the following: Does the community have clear guidelines? Are discussions respectful and inclusive? Do you feel comfortable sharing your experiences? Use these observations to decide whether this community aligns with your values and needs. This reflection can guide you in finding a supportive and welcoming online environment.

6.2 CREATING LOCAL SUPPORT NETWORKS

Imagine a space where you can connect face-to-face with others who share similar experiences and challenges, a place where understanding flows naturally and support is readily available. Establishing local support networks can be a vital step in achieving this sense of community. The first step is to identify local resources that cater to the needs of autistic adults. Every community is different, but in many areas, community centers sometimes have programs specifically designed for people with autism. These centers might offer social groups, workshops, or recreational activities tailored to different interests and needs. Libraries can also serve as valuable resources. In larger communities, they may host autism-friendly events like book clubs or discussion groups. These events can provide a relaxed environment in which to meet others and engage in shared activities. Reach out to these establishments to learn more about their offerings and how you might get involved.

Building collaborative relationships with local organizations can further strengthen your support network. Schools and universities often have resources and programs designed to support autistic individuals. Collaborating with these institutions can lead to mutually beneficial partnerships. Consider co-hosting events or workshops with their support, leveraging their facilities and expertise to reach a wider audience. Engaging with local advocacy groups can also provide valuable opportunities for collaboration. These groups may offer resources, expertise, and networks that can enhance your initiatives. Working together, you can create comprehensive support systems that address the diverse needs of the autistic community. Partnerships not only expand the reach of your efforts but also lead to a greater sense of unity and shared purpose. Your community may or may not have these types of resources, but it is well worth exploring options.

Sustaining support networks requires ongoing effort and commitment. Regularly scheduled meetings help maintain momentum and keep participants engaged. Establish a consistent schedule, whether it's monthly, bi-weekly, or weekly, to ensure everyone knows when and where to gather. Consistency builds trust and reliability, encouraging continued participation. Feedback loops are essential for continuous improvement and adaptation. Encourage participants to share their thoughts and suggestions on how to enhance the network. This feedback can guide future planning and ensure that the network remains relevant and responsive to the community's needs. Consider creating a dedicated channel, such as an email list or online forum, for ongoing communication and feedback. This allows for transparent dialogue and encourages a collaborative atmosphere.

If you're feeling particularly proactive, you could also organize meetups and gatherings yourself. Not everyone is inclined to do that, but don't dismiss it out of hand. Begin by choosing accessible venues that are welcoming and accommodating to all participants. Consider factors such as location, transportation options, and sensory-friendly environments when selecting a venue. Once you have a location, plan inclusive activities that cater to a wide range of interests and abilities. This might include board game nights, art workshops, or outdoor picnics. The goal is to create an environment where everyone feels comfortable and included. Promoting your meetups through local channels such as community bulletin boards, social media, or word-of-mouth can help attract participants. Utilize platforms like Meetup.com to reach a broader audience and ensure your events are well-attended. Consistent promotion and engagement can help build momentum and encourage regular participation.

Inclusive and supportive networks thrive on the active involvement of their members. Encourage participants to take on roles within the network, whether it's organizing events, leading discussions, or managing communications. This collective effort strengthens the community and ensures its sustainability. Continuously seek opportunities for growth and expansion, exploring new partnerships and initiatives that align with your goals. By nurturing these relationships and networks, you create a resilient and supportive community that can adapt and evolve to meet the changing needs of its members. Additionally, engaging in advocacy activities has the dual purpose of creating a community for yourself as well as helping the broader neurodivergent community. We explore the subject of advocacy in depth in Chapter 8.

6.3 UTILIZING COMMUNITY RESOURCES

When you're navigating the world as an adult with autism, finding the right support can make all the difference. Communities are rich with resources tailored to meet diverse needs. Specialized counseling services offer a space where your unique experiences are understood and validated. These services often employ therapists trained to address the specific challenges faced by autistic individuals, providing strategies for managing stress, improving communication, and enhancing overall well-being. Counseling can be a cornerstone of support, offering individualized guidance and a safe space to explore personal challenges and growth. Additionally, some communities provide workshops and educational programs. These programs can range from skill-building workshops focused on employment readiness to educational seminars that delve into topics like executive functioning or sensory management. Attending these programs can equip you with practical skills and knowledge, fostering confidence and independence.

To make the most of available community resources, it's important to approach them with intention and planning. Start by scheduling consultations and appointments with service providers. This not only ensures that you receive the support you need but also allows you to assess whether a particular resource is the right fit for you. Be proactive in joining resource mailing lists, as these often offer updates on new workshops, support groups, and events. These alerts can keep you informed about opportunities to further your personal and professional development. Engaging regularly with these resources can lead to new insights and connections, enhancing your community involvement and personal growth.

Evaluating the quality of resources is crucial to ensure they meet your needs effectively. Begin by reading reviews and testimonials from others who have used these services. Their experiences can provide valuable insights into the strengths and weaknesses of a resource. Look for feedback on aspects such as the professionalism of staff, the relevance of content, and the overall impact on participants. Additionally, you can seek recommendations from peers within the autistic community. Their firsthand experiences can guide you toward resources that have proven beneficial. Word-of-mouth referrals often carry weight because they reflect genuine satisfaction and trust. By evaluating resources thoroughly, you can choose those that will contribute most positively to your journey.

Advocating to improve resources is an empowering way to enhance the support available in your community. Participate in community surveys to provide feedback on your experiences with various services. These surveys often guide future developments and improvements, which help those resources better meet the needs of the community. Engaging in discussions with resource providers can also have an impact. Share your insights and suggestions directly with those who offer these services. This dialogue can lead to meaningful changes, such as the introduction of new programs or the refinement of existing ones. By advocating for improvements, you not only enhance your experience but also contribute to the betterment of the community as a whole.

Interactive Element: Creating a Resource Evaluation Checklist

Develop a personal checklist for evaluating community resources to help you systematically assess their effectiveness. Consider including criteria such as accessibility, relevance, staff expertise, and user feedback. Use this checklist to guide your exploration of resources, ensuring you choose those best suited to your needs. This tool can be a practical aid in navigating the options available, empowering you to make informed decisions about the support you seek. Not all communities will have the same level of resources, but the criteria to assess them are the same.

In many ways, the resources available to autistic adults within communities are like a toolkit. They're filled with options and opportunities designed to support your unique path. From specialized counseling to educational workshops, these resources are there to uplift and assist you. By actively engaging with and evaluating these resources, you can build a network of support that aligns with your personal goals and needs. And by advocating for improvements, you contribute to a cycle of growth and enhancement, not only for yourself but for the entire community.

6.4 BUILDING INCLUSIVE ENVIRONMENTS

Creating an inclusive environment is about more than just making spaces accessible; it's about encouraging a culture where diverse needs and perspectives are understood and valued. For autistic individuals, this means recognizing that each person's sensory, communication, and social preferences may differ. Inclusivity involves encouraging open-mindedness and acceptance, allowing individuals to express themselves without fear of judgment or exclusion. It's important to approach inclusivity with a mindset that embraces diversity, seeing it as a strength that enriches the community rather than a challenge to be managed. This perspective is vital in building spaces that cater to the unique needs of autistic individuals, ensuring they feel seen and heard.

As an adult with autism, you are uniquely qualified to understand and address the specific needs of autistic individuals. One practical approach to improving inclusive practices is to conduct training sessions on autism awareness. These sessions can educate community members, staff, and volunteers about autism, providing insights into the diverse ways it can manifest. By increasing awareness, these trainings help dispel myths and reduce stigma, paving the way for more informed interactions. Creating accessibility plans is another option. These plans should outline strategies for accommodating various sensory and communication needs, such as providing quiet areas, offering visual support, and using clear, direct language. You may find yourself with the opportunity to provide such training, either alone or in partnership with another.

You can ensure diverse voices are heard simply by participating in community discourse. Being part of an advisory panel can provide valuable insights into the needs and preferences of the autistic community. These panels can guide initiatives and projects and ensure they align with the interests and priorities of autistic individuals. Participating in, or even hosting, inclusive community forums is another effective strategy. These forums offer a platform for open dialogue, allowing community members to share their experiences, ideas, and concerns. By involving a wide range of voices, these forums can inform policies and practices that reflect the community's diversity. This collaborative approach not only empowers individuals but also strengthens the community as a whole, creating an environment where everyone feels valued and respected.

Celebrating diversity within communities is about recognizing and appreciating the unique contributions of each individual. Cultural and awareness events provide opportunities to highlight the richness of diverse experiences, which leads to a sense of pride and connection. These events can include art exhibitions, performances, and workshops that showcase the talents and stories of autistic individuals. By celebrating diversity, communities can promote understanding and empathy, breaking down barriers and building bridges between different groups. Showcasing diverse talents and contributions is another powerful way to celebrate diversity. Whether through public displays, publications, or digital platforms, highlighting the achievements of autistic individuals can inspire others and challenge stereotypes. These celebrations not only honor individual successes but also reinforce the message that diversity is an asset to be cherished and embraced.

As we look to the future, the focus will shift toward practical daily living skills, exploring strategies and tools to enhance independence and well-being in everyday life. This next chapter will delve into the practical aspects of daily living, offering insights and guidance to support your journey toward greater autonomy and fulfillment.

SEVEN

PRACTICAL DAILY LIVING SKILLS

I magine waking up each day with a clear plan, where every task finds its place and every moment aligns with your natural rhythm. For many adults with autism, managing daily tasks can feel like piecing together a complex puzzle. Yet, with the right tools and strategies, this puzzle can transform into a map that guides you through your day with confidence and clarity. This chapter delves into practical tools and techniques to help you organize your life, focusing on executive functioning and daily routine consistency.

7.1 ORGANIZING DAILY TASKS WITH EXECUTIVE FUNCTION TOOLS

We discussed tools to manage executive function at the workplace in Chapter 4. The same tools can be used in other areas of life, as well. These task management tools offer a lifeline to those grappling with executive dysfunction, providing structure and clarity where there might otherwise be chaos.

As we discussed in Chapter 4, digital apps like Todoist and Trello can be particularly helpful, offering a platform to organize tasks visually and set reminders. Todoist, for instance, allows you to categorize tasks by priority and deadline, ensuring nothing slips through the cracks. Trello, on the other hand, uses boards and cards to visually map out projects, making it easier to track progress and collaborate with others if needed. For those who prefer tangible aids, physical planners or bullet journals provide a hands-on approach to task management. These tools encourage you to engage with your tasks actively, offering a sense of satisfaction as you check off completed items. By integrating these tools into your routine, you create a framework that supports your unique way of thinking and working.

Visual schedules can further simplify task management by providing a clear, at-a-glance overview of your day, week, or month. Color-coded calendars, whether digital or physical, offer a vibrant way to distinguish between different types of activities or priorities, allowing you to quickly assess what lies ahead. For example, you might use green for work-related tasks, blue for social activities, and red for self-care. This color-coding system can make it easier to balance various aspects of life, ensuring that you allocate time appropriately for each. Visual task boards, similar to those used in Trello, can also be recreated physically with sticky notes or index cards, offering a tactile method to organize tasks. By arranging tasks visually, you can better plan your day, identifying which activities need immediate attention and which can wait. My personal favorite method is to write on a whiteboard with a set of colored markers. I like the unlined space, which lets me diagram tasks spacially rather than write them out linearly. Take the time to find what works best for you.

Routine consistency can also be key to managing daily tasks effectively, providing a predictable structure that supports executive functioning. Developing morning and evening rituals can set the tone for your day, helping you transition smoothly between different activities. A morning ritual might include a set time for breakfast, a brief meditation session, or a review of your day's tasks. An evening ritual could involve winding down with a book, preparing for the next day, or reflecting on accomplishments. Weekly review and planning sessions offer an opportunity to assess the previous week's successes and challenges, adjusting your approach as needed. These sessions help you maintain oversight of your tasks, ensuring that your routine remains aligned with your goals and needs.

Incorporating these strategies into your daily life can significantly enhance your ability to manage tasks, reducing stress and increasing productivity. By understanding executive functioning, utilizing task management tools, creating visual schedules, and developing routine consistency, you can improve your experience of daily living.

Interactive Element: Executive Function Checklist

Create a checklist to identify areas where you might face challenges with executive functioning. Consider including categories like task initiation, prioritization, and time management. Reflect on which tasks you find difficult and note any patterns. Use this checklist to guide your selection of tools and strategies, ensuring they address your specific needs. This personalized approach can empower you to tackle daily tasks with greater confidence and success.

7.2 COOKING AND MEAL PLANNING FOR SENSORY PREFERENCES

Navigating the culinary world with sensory preferences can be a unique challenge for autistic adults. The way textures and flavors interact on your palate can significantly influence your food choices and overall dining experience. Some individuals might find the crunch of raw vegetables too overwhelming, while others might avoid certain textures like creamy or slimy foods altogether. Flavor sensitivities also play a critical role; even a hint of spice or bitterness can be off-putting, leading to a limited range of acceptable foods. Understanding these preferences is vital to creating meals that are both enjoyable and nutritious. By identifying specific aversions and preferences, you can tailor your meal planning to ensure each dish aligns with your sensory needs, making dining a more enjoyable experience.

Factoring in your sensory preferences can significantly reduce the stress of meal planning. Rotating favorite meals within your weekly menu can offer comfort and familiarity, reducing anxiety around mealtime. This strategy not only simplifies decision-making but also ensures that you have a reliable set of dishes that cater to your taste and texture preferences. Incorporating sensory-friendly ingredients is another practical approach. This might include choosing softer grains like quinoa or couscous, which can be more palatable if you have a sensitivity to chewy textures. You might also opt for naturally sweet vegetables like carrots or sweet potatoes, which can provide flavor without overwhelming your senses. By thoughtfully selecting ingredients that align with your sensory preferences, you can create meals that are both nourishing and enjoyable.

Simple and adaptive recipes can be a lifesaver for those with specific sensory preferences. Smoothies and blended soups are excellent options, offering a smooth texture that is easy to customize. You can adjust the thickness, sweetness, or flavor profile to suit your needs, ensuring each sip is just right. Customizable stir-fry dishes allow for flexibility with ingredients, letting you include only those textures and flavors you find acceptable. The beauty of a stir-fry lies in its adaptability; you can adjust the level of softness or crispness by altering cooking times or methods. Similarly, build-your-own salad bars can provide a tailored dining experience, allowing you to choose only the toppings and dressings that meet your sensory criteria. These recipes not only accommodate your preferences but also encourage creativity and exploration in the kitchen.

Grocery shopping can often feel overwhelming, but with the right strategies, it can become a more manageable task. Creating a detailed shopping list is an effective way to streamline the process. By listing items by category, such as produce, dairy, or grains, you simplify the shopping experience and reduce the likelihood of forgetting essential ingredients. Additionally, using delivery services can alleviate the stress of navigating crowded stores by delivering your groceries directly to your door. This service can be invaluable if you have specific brands or products that cater to your sensory needs, ensuring you always have access to your preferred items. Shopping during off-peak hours is another way to make the experience more pleasant. Fewer crowds mean less noise and a calmer environment, allowing you to focus on selecting the right products without added stress. These strategies can transform grocery shopping from a daunting chore to a straightforward part of your weekly routine.

Cooking and meal planning for sensory preferences is about creating an environment that respects your unique needs and enhances mealtimes. By understanding how textures and flavors influence your food choices, you can plan meals that accommodate your preferences, ensuring each bite is enjoyable. Simple, adaptive recipes offer flexibility, allowing you to tailor dishes to your liking, while thoughtful grocery shopping strategies streamline the process, reducing stress and ensuring you have the ingredients you need. With these tools and insights, you can navigate the kitchen with confidence, creating meals that nourish both body and mind.

7.3 FINANCIAL MANAGEMENT: BUDGETING AND PLANNING

Understanding financial basics is a crucial element of daily living, as it lays the groundwork for managing your resources effectively. Budgeting and expense tracking are at the heart of this, as they give you a clear picture of where your money goes each month. Budgeting involves setting up a plan that allocates your income towards essentials like housing, utilities, and food while considering discretionary spending on entertainment or hobbies. Tracking expenses, meanwhile, helps you understand your spending habits, allowing you to adjust as needed. This process is essential for maintaining financial stability and avoiding unnecessary debt.

There are a few key steps to creating a budget that can help you manage your finances with confidence. Start by categorizing your expenses into fixed and variable costs. Fixed expenses, like rent or mortgage payments, remain constant each month, whereas variable expenses, such as groceries or dining out, can fluctuate. Categorizing these expenses provides clarity, helping you identify areas where you can cut back if needed. Once you have a clear picture of your spending, you can set individual financial goals. These goals might include saving for a vacation, building an emergency fund, or paying off debt. Having specific goals can motivate you to stick to your budget, providing a sense of purpose and direction. Budgeting apps like Mint can simplify this process, offering tools to track expenses, set goals, and monitor your progress. These apps provide a user-friendly interface, making it easier to manage your finances without feeling overwhelmed.

Staying on top of bills and payments is one essential aspect of financial management. Setting up automatic payments can be an effective strategy, as it ensures bills are paid on time without requiring constant attention. Many banks and service providers offer this option, allowing you to link your accounts and schedule regular payments. This automation reduces the risk of missed payments, providing peace of mind. Additionally, using reminders and alerts can help you stay organized. Set up notifications on your phone or computer to remind you of upcoming due dates, making sure you have ample time to make arrangements if needed. These reminders can be beneficial for variable expenses, like credit card payments, which may differ each month. By staying proactive, you can maintain a healthy financial standing, avoiding the stress and financial penalties associated with late payments.

Building financial resilience involves developing habits that promote long-term stability and security. One of the most effective ways to build resilience is by establishing an emergency savings fund. This fund acts as a financial cushion, providing resources for unexpected expenses like medical bills or car repairs. An ideal target is to save enough to cover three to six months of living expenses, which you can gradually build over time. Having a robust emergency fund can reduce anxiety because you will have the means to handle unforeseen challenges without disrupting your financial stability. Planning for irregular expenses is equally important, as it prevents these costs from derailing your budget. Consider setting aside a portion of your income for annual expenses like insurance premiums, vehicle maintenance, or holiday gifts. By anticipating these costs and incorporating them into your financial plan, you can avoid the stress of scrambling for funds when they arise.

Developing strong financial habits takes time and effort, but the rewards are significant. By understanding the basics of budgeting and expense tracking, creating a personal budget, managing bills and payments, and building financial resilience, you can take control of your finances and work towards your goals. These practices not only provide a sense of security but also empower you to make informed decisions, helping to maintain your financial well-being.

7.4 NAVIGATING TRANSPORTATION AND TRAVEL

Understanding your transportation options can significantly impact how you manage travel. Public transit, such as buses and trains, offers cost-effective solutions and reduces the stress of driving in busy areas. However, it can also pose challenges like crowded spaces and unpredictable schedules, which might lead to sensory overload. On the other hand, personal vehicles provide a controlled environment, allowing you to adjust settings like temperature and music to your preference. This control can be comforting, yet owning a car comes with responsibilities such as maintenance and insurance costs. Ride-sharing services like Uber or Lyft offer flexibility and convenience, especially in urban areas, without the long-term commitment of owning a car. These services can be helpful for short trips or when public transit isn't accessible. Each option has its pros and cons, and choosing the right one depends on your personal needs and preferences.

When planning travel routes, efficiency and low stress are key. Apps like Google Maps can be indispensable tools, offering real-time traffic updates and alternative routes to avoid congestion. These apps can help you plan your journey, providing estimated travel times and directions. Identifying sensory-friendly travel times can also make a significant difference. For instance, traveling during off-peak hours can mean less crowded trains or buses, which can be more manageable if you are sensitive to noise or crowds. Preparing for potential delays is equally important. Build extra time into your schedule to accommodate unexpected disruptions, reducing anxiety about arriving late. This buffer can provide peace of mind, allowing you to approach travel with greater confidence and flexibility. Planning thoughtfully can help your travel experience be as smooth and stress-free as possible.

Travel anxiety is a common challenge, but several techniques can help ease these feelings. Visualization exercises are a powerful tool, enabling you to mentally walk through each step of the journey before it happens. Picture yourself calmly arriving at the station, boarding the train, and reaching your destination. This mental rehearsal can reduce uncertainty and make the process feel more familiar and manageable. Travel checklists are another good strategy. Listing everything you need to do and bring helps to make sure everything is remembered, providing a tangible guide to follow. This preparation can alleviate stress, allowing you to focus on the experience itself rather than worrying about logistics. By incorporating these techniques into your travel routine, you can reduce anxiety and approach each trip with greater ease and confidence.

Packing efficiently can help you travel more comfortably. Start by organizing luggage for easy access and placing essentials like snacks, water, and entertainment within reach. Consider using packing cubes to separate items, making it easier to find what you need without rummaging through your bag. Packing sensory tools and comfort items can make a significant difference, particularly on longer journeys. Noise-canceling headphones can block out overwhelming sounds, while a favorite fidget toy or weighted blanket can provide comfort and stability. These items create a personal bubble of calm, helping you manage sensory input and maintain focus. By packing thoughtfully, you ensure that your travel experience is comfortable and enjoyable, with everything you need close at hand.

Over the years, I have discovered a particular style of hand luggage that works best for me. I have a specific compartment where I store each comfort and entertainment aid. This bag is a familiar travel companion for me and helps me locate the items I may want quickly and predictably. If you find something that works for you, consider replicating it for each trip, making it a comforting, reliable accessory.

7.5 MANAGING CHANGE AND ROUTINE DISRUPTIONS

Change is a constant in life, yet for autistic individuals, it can be particularly daunting. The very nature of change disrupts the predictability and routine that often serve as a comforting anchor. When routines are altered, it can lead to an emotional and sensory upheaval. A sudden change might feel like stepping into a whirlwind, where familiar cues are lost in the chaos. This can trigger heightened anxiety as the brain scrambles to adapt to new stimuli without its usual frameworks in place. Understanding the impact of change is crucial because it underscores the importance of developing strategies to manage these disruptions effectively. Flexibility and adaptation become essential tools in navigating these shifts. While the initial response to change might be discomfort, cultivating flexibility allows for a smoother transition from the known to the unknown, transforming potential chaos into a manageable, albeit different, order.

Developing coping mechanisms to handle unexpected changes can significantly alleviate stress. Practicing mindfulness during change can serve as an anchor, grounding you in the present moment. Mindfulness involves focusing on your breath, acknowledging your feelings, and observing them without judgment. This practice can help calm the mind, reducing the emotional intensity of change. Creating backup plans offers another layer of security. By anticipating potential disruptions and having alternative actions ready, you reduce the uncertainty that change can bring. For instance, if a planned event is canceled, having a list of other activities you enjoy can fill the sudden void. These strategies provide a sense of control, empowering you to handle disruptions with confidence, knowing that you have the tools to navigate them.

Maintaining routine flexibility is about embracing the ebb and flow of daily life while preserving a sense of order. Allowing buffer time for transitions is a practical strategy that can ease the shift from one activity to another. This might mean scheduling extra time between appointments or giving yourself a set time to decompress after work before diving into evening activities. Incorporating flexible activities into your routine can also help. Choose activities that can be easily adapted or rescheduled, offering a sense of continuity even when other plans change. For instance, having a list of favorite pastimes that require little preparation, like a walk in the park or reading a book, ensures that you always have options that fit within your day, regardless of unexpected changes. This flexibility supports a dynamic routine, one that adapts to life's unpredictability without losing its core structure.

Building resilience to change involves gradually exposing yourself to new experiences and reflecting on past successful adaptations. Start small by introducing minor changes to your routine, such as taking a different route to a familiar destination or trying a new hobby. These small shifts can build confidence, demonstrating that change, while initially uncomfortable, can lead to positive outcomes. Reflecting on past experiences where you successfully adapted to change can also bolster resilience. Consider moments when you navigated disruptions effectively and identify the strategies that helped you succeed. This reflection reinforces your ability to handle change, providing a blueprint for future challenges. By embracing these practices, you strengthen your capacity to adapt, transforming change from a source of anxiety to an opportunity for growth.

As we conclude this chapter, remember that managing change and routine disruptions is an ongoing process. The strategies we've explored—understanding the impact of change, developing coping mechanisms, maintaining routine flexibility, and building resilience—equip you with tools to navigate life's inevitable shifts. While change may never be entirely comfortable, these practices can transform it into a manageable and even enriching aspect of life. Looking ahead, we will explore how these skills intersect with the broader context of empowerment and advocacy, focusing on how you can use your strengths to create a fulfilling and authentic life.

EIGHT
EMPOWERMENT AND ADVOCACY

Picture yourself in a bustling café. The chatter of conversations, the clinking of cups, and the hum of an espresso machine create a vibrant symphony. Amidst this, you speak up to request a quieter corner. This seemingly small act embodies self-advocacy, a powerful tool that enables you to navigate the world with confidence and assertiveness. Self-advocacy is about knowing your needs and expressing them effectively so that your environment aligns with your well-being. It is a crucial skill for adults with autism, who often face systems designed around neurotypical norms.

8.1 SELF ADVOCACY

Understanding self-advocacy involves recognizing its significance in daily life. For autistic individuals, it means effectively communicating your wants, needs, and rights to secure necessary accommodations. This might include requesting adjustments in work settings, explaining sensory preferences to friends, or advocating for healthcare that respects your sensory sensitivities. Everyday self-advocacy actions, like asking for more time to process information during conversations or seeking a quiet space in a public area, empower you to create an environment where you feel comfortable and understood. These actions might seem minor, but they contribute significantly to feeling personally empowered. They reinforce your autonomy and sovereignty, highlighting your ability to shape your surroundings to meet your needs better.

Developing the skills to advocate for yourself is essential for navigating a world often ill-equipped to accommodate neurodiversity. Practicing assertive communication is one of those key skills. Assertive communication involves expressing your thoughts clearly and respectfully without diminishing your needs or the perspectives of others. You could practice this through role-playing scenarios, where you rehearse how to articulate your needs in various situations. For instance, you might simulate a conversation with an employer about workplace accommodations, focusing on maintaining clarity and confidence. These exercises build your comfort with expressing your needs, preparing you for real-world interactions where advocacy is necessary. Role-playing can also help address social cues, ensuring your message is communicated effectively.

Despite its importance, self-advocacy can feel challenging. Fear of confrontation is a common barrier; the prospect of disagreement or misunderstanding can deter you from speaking up. Overcoming this fear involves reframing confrontation as a constructive dialogue rather than a conflict. Approach these conversations with the mindset that advocating for your needs benefits everyone involved, leading to clearer communication and understanding. Self-doubt and uncertainty can also hinder advocacy efforts. It's crucial to remember that your needs are valid, and expressing them is an essential part of self-care. Building confidence in your advocacy skills can be gradual. Start with small, low-stakes situations to practice voicing your needs, gradually working up to more complex interactions as your confidence grows.

Sometimes, a powerful advocacy tool can be as simple as sharing your personal story. Your experiences can provide insight and perspective that statistics and data alone cannot convey. Creating content for blogs or social media allows you to reach a broad audience, sharing your journey and the challenges and triumphs along the way. By telling your story, you humanize the issues faced by autistic individuals, which can lead to increased understanding and empathy. You may even feel called to public speaking. Speaking at events and conferences is another way to share your narrative that can break down barriers and dispel myths. Your voice is unique, and sharing your experiences can contribute to a richer, more inclusive dialogue. Everyone has a different comfort level when speaking (or writing) publicly, so be gentle with yourself and experiment with this as you feel comfortable.

The benefits of self-advocacy create a ripple effect that extends beyond yourself. When you share your successes in this area, you inspire others to recognize their potential to be their own best advocate. Your experiences provide a roadmap for peers navigating similar challenges and can help them develop effective strategies and approaches. Leading by example, you contribute to a culture of empowerment and support within the autistic community. Sharing resources, such as advocacy toolkits or personal strategies, enriches the collective knowledge and strengthens the community's capacity for self-advocacy. This collaborative approach not only enhances individual empowerment but also leads to a sense of solidarity and shared purpose.

Reflection Section: Personal Advocacy Journal

Consider keeping a personal advocacy journal to document your self-advocacy experiences. Record situations where you successfully advocated for your needs, noting the strategies that worked well and any challenges you encountered. Reflect on how these experiences made you feel and what you learned. This journal can serve as a valuable resource, highlighting your growth in advocating for yourself and providing inspiration for future interactions.

You could share your journal with trusted peers or mentors. Their feedback could offer new perspectives and ideas to refine your advocacy skills further. By documenting your journey, you create a tangible record of your empowerment, reinforcing the importance of these skills in your daily life.

8.2 STRATEGIES FOR COMMUNITY ENGAGEMENT

As discussed, engaging with the autism community can be both rewarding and transformative, offering opportunities to connect with others and contribute to a more inclusive society. First, identify opportunities in your community, such as volunteering with local autism organizations. These organizations often welcome volunteers who can offer unique insights and experiences. By participating, you not only support important causes but also build relationships with others who understand the nuances of autism. Additional opportunities to engage are community events and forums. They provide spaces where you can share your perspectives and learn from others. These gatherings often focus on topics relevant to autism and neurodiversity, creating environments conducive to meaningful discussions and connections.

Another way to participate is by joining national and local advocacy groups. In the USA, organizations like the Autistic Self Advocacy Network (ASAN) provide opportunities to engage in meaningful advocacy work. These groups often organize campaigns, events, and initiatives that aim to influence public policy and raise awareness. Participating in awareness campaigns can be an impactful way to contribute. These campaigns focus on educating the public about autism and celebrating neurodiversity, and giving you the opportunity to connect with others.

Building collaborative relationships within your community can increase your impact. Working with local businesses to promote inclusive practices is an excellent starting point. Businesses that recognize the value of diversity often seek partnerships with individuals who can advise on creating welcoming environments for all customers. By collaborating with these businesses, you can help implement changes that make a difference. Educators and schools are also key allies. Collaborating with them to develop programs that support autistic students can foster more inclusive educational settings. Sharing your experiences and knowledge can help educators understand the unique needs of autistic individuals, leading to better support and resources within schools. These partnerships not only benefit the immediate community but also contribute to a broader culture of acceptance and inclusivity.

Initiating and leading community projects is another powerful way to engage. Organizing awareness campaigns can bring attention to important issues and promote understanding. These campaigns might involve hosting informational sessions, creating online content, or distributing materials that educate the public about autism. Developing support groups or workshops is another avenue to consider. These groups provide safe spaces for individuals to share their experiences and support one another. Workshops can focus on specific skills or topics, such as stress management or communication techniques, offering practical solutions and insights. By taking the lead in these initiatives, you create opportunities for growth and connection, empowering others to engage with the community in meaningful ways. Not everyone feels inclined to take on a leadership role. That is fine, but keep an open mind. People evolve in different ways.

Measuring the success of a community engagement effort is an important metric. Collecting feedback from participants can provide valuable insights into what worked well and what might be improved. Surveys, interviews, or informal conversations can all be effective methods for gathering this feedback. Tracking changes in community awareness is another way to assess impact. This might involve monitoring engagement on social media platforms, observing increased participation in events, or noting shifts in public discussions about autism. These measures can help you understand the reach and effectiveness of your efforts, guiding future initiatives and ensuring that they continue to resonate with and benefit the community.

8.3 ADVOCATING FOR NEURODIVERSITY IN SOCIETY

Neurodiversity is a concept that recognizes neurological differences as natural variations of the human mind. It challenges the traditional view that frames these differences primarily as deficits. Instead, it promotes the idea that conditions like autism, ADHD, and dyslexia are part of natural diversity, bringing unique strengths and perspectives. Recognizing neurodiversity as a natural variation invites society to embrace these differences, seeing them as essential contributions to human diversity. In doing so, we begin to dismantle societal norms and stereotypes that often marginalize neurodivergent individuals. This shift is crucial in creating a society that values all forms of cognition, challenging the outdated stereotypes that have long dictated how neurodivergent individuals are perceived and treated.

Raising public awareness about neurodiversity is a vital step that will benefit those on the autism spectrum and those who are not. If you feel so inclined, engaging in public speaking opportunities is an effective strategy. Sharing your experiences and insights can educate others, break down misconceptions, and foster understanding. Whether speaking at local events, schools, or professional gatherings, these engagements provide a platform to highlight the importance of embracing neurodiversity. Creating educational materials and presentations is another powerful approach. These resources can be distributed at libraries, community centers, or online. They serve as accessible tools for those seeking to learn more about neurodiversity, offering insights into the strengths and needs of neurodivergent individuals. By reaching a broad audience, you contribute to a more informed and empathetic society.

Collaborating with allies is essential in advancing the cause of neurodiversity. Partnering with neurotypical advocates can enhance efforts to promote understanding. Allies can amplify your message, providing support and resources that may be out of reach otherwise. Forming alliances with diversity-focused organizations is equally important. These groups often have established networks and platforms that can help elevate discussions around neurodiversity. Working together creates a united front, strengthening advocacy efforts and driving change more effectively. These collaborations not only broaden the reach of your message but also demonstrate the power of collective action. By building a network of allies, you create a more robust movement that can influence societal attitudes and policies.

Promoting inclusive policies is a crucial aspect of advocating for neurodiversity. Engaging in policy discussions and forums allows you to voice the needs of neurodivergent individuals in legislative settings. These discussions are opportunities to highlight areas where current policies may fall short and propose changes that better accommodate diverse needs. Lobbying for legislative changes is a practical way to advocate for systemic improvements. This might involve working with advocacy groups to draft proposals, meeting with lawmakers to discuss your concerns, or participating in public hearings. By advocating for policy changes, you help create a legal framework that supports neurodiversity, ensuring that the needs of all individuals are considered and respected.

Interactive Element: Creating Your Advocacy Toolkit

Consider developing a personal advocacy toolkit to support your efforts in promoting neurodiversity. This toolkit might include brochures or flyers explaining the principles of neurodiversity, templates for letters to policymakers, and guides for organizing community events. Having these resources readily available can streamline your advocacy work, making it easier to respond to opportunities as they arise. Additionally, you can share your toolkit with others, empowering them to join the cause. By equipping yourself and others with the right tools, you strengthen the movement for neurodiversity, creating a ripple effect that extends throughout society.

Advocating for neurodiversity in society requires a multifaceted approach that combines education, collaboration, and policy change. By embracing the principles of neurodiversity, raising public awareness, collaborating with allies, and promoting inclusive policies, you contribute to a world that values all forms of human diversity. Your efforts help create an environment where neurodivergent individuals can thrive, free from the constraints of outdated stereotypes and barriers. As you continue this important work, remember that each step you take contributes to a larger movement. Together, we can build a more inclusive and accepting society, one that celebrates the unique contributions of every individual, regardless of their neurological makeup.

8.4 CRAFTING YOUR PERSONAL ADVOCACY PLAN

Imagine standing at the threshold of a new path, one where your voice leads the way in shaping a world more attuned to your needs and those of others like you. Crafting a personal advocacy plan begins with setting clear and achievable goals. These goals act as a compass, guiding your actions and ensuring your efforts lead to meaningful change. Start by identifying specific areas where you want to make an impact—perhaps accessibility in public spaces or increased awareness in workplaces. Once you have pinpointed these areas, distinguish between short-term and long-term objectives. Short-term goals might include attending a local meeting or speaking with a manager about workplace adjustments. Long-term goals could involve broader initiatives, such as contributing to policy changes or launching community programs. Prioritizing these objectives helps keep your plan focused and actionable, ensuring that each step you take builds towards a larger vision.

Developing a strategic plan tailored to your strengths is the next crucial step. This plan should map out actionable steps that align with your capabilities and resources. Begin by breaking down each goal into smaller, manageable tasks. For instance, if your aim is to enhance workplace inclusivity, start by researching best practices and gathering supporting data. Allocate time and resources wisely —perhaps dedicating a few hours each week to advocacy efforts or setting aside a small budget for materials and travel. Consider your personal strengths and how they can be leveraged in your plan. Whether it's strong communication skills, a knack for organizing, or an ability to connect with others, these strengths are assets that can drive your advocacy forward. By creating a plan that plays to your abilities, you increase the likelihood of success and maintain motivation throughout the process.

Utilizing advocacy tools and resources can significantly bolster your efforts. Advocacy toolkits and guides, such as those provided by organizations like Autism Speaks, offer valuable insights into effective strategies and techniques. These resources often include templates for letters, guides for public speaking, and tips for engaging with policymakers. Online platforms also serve as powerful tools for advocacy campaigns. Websites and social media channels can amplify your message, reaching a broader audience and engaging supporters. Through these platforms, you can share stories, disseminate information, and mobilize others to join your cause. By incorporating these tools into your plan, you enhance your ability to effect change and connect with a network of like-minded individuals.

Evaluating your progress is a valuable tool for maintaining momentum and ensuring your efforts remain effective. Regular reflection allows you to assess both successes and challenges, providing insights into what is working and where adjustments may be needed. You could keep a journal to track your activities, outcomes, and reflections. This practice not only documents your journey but also highlights patterns and areas for improvement. Making iterative improvements based on this evaluation helps refine your plan over time. For example, if a particular approach isn't yielding the desired results, explore alternative strategies or seek feedback from peers. Flexibility and adaptability are key, allowing you to navigate obstacles and seize new opportunities as they arise. By continuously refining your plan, you ensure it remains aligned with your evolving goals and the changing landscape of advocacy.

The process of crafting a personal advocacy plan empowers you to take control of your advocacy journey. It provides a structured framework that guides your actions and keeps you focused on your objectives. By setting clear goals, developing a strategic plan, utilizing available tools, and evaluating your progress, you can maximize your impact and contribute meaningfully to the causes you care about. This approach not only enhances your personal advocacy efforts but also inspires others to engage in similar pursuits, creating a ripple effect of positive change within your community and beyond.

8.5 CELEBRATING NEURODIVERSITY: EMBRACING DIFFERENCES

Celebrating neurodiversity means highlighting and including the voices and experiences of autistic individuals from all walks of life. Each story shared enriches our collective understanding of what it means to navigate the world with a unique perspective. These stories should feature people from different cultural and gender perspectives, as these narratives highlight the diverse ways autism is experienced and expressed. An autistic person from a rural background may have vastly different experiences compared to someone living in a bustling city, just as sexual and gender identity shapes one's interactions and challenges. Similarly, many individuals with autism have other concurrent neurodiversities, such as ADHD or other configurations.

Showcasing artistic and academic contributions can be very effective. Autistic individuals often bring innovative ideas and remarkable talent to their fields, whether it's through captivating art, groundbreaking research, or insightful writing. By highlighting these achievements, we not only celebrate individual contributions but also challenge stereotypes, showing the world the richness and depth of the autistic community.

Creating events that celebrate neurodiversity provides opportunities for the autistic community to gather, share, and learn. Planning autism acceptance festivals can bring together individuals, families, and allies in a vibrant celebration of diversity. These festivals might include performances, workshops, and panel discussions, creating a space where autistic voices are front and center. Hosting inclusive art exhibitions offers another avenue for celebration. Art has the power to communicate experiences and emotions in ways words sometimes cannot, making it a particularly effective medium for showcasing the diverse expressions of neurodiversity. These exhibitions not only highlight the artistic talents of autistic individuals but also offer audiences a new lens through which to view the world.

Celebratory events also serve as educational opportunities. By inviting guest speakers to share their insights and experiences, these events can foster deeper understanding and empathy. Workshops focused on specific topics, such as sensory processing or communication strategies, can provide attendees with practical tools and knowledge. Distributing educational materials at events ensures that the information shared is accessible to a broader audience, encouraging continued learning beyond the event itself. These materials might include brochures, articles, or links to online resources that attendees can explore at their own pace. By combining celebration with education, these events create a dynamic environment where learning and joy coexist.

A cultural shift toward embracing differences requires more than isolated events; it calls for an ongoing commitment to creating a culture of acceptance. Every open conversation about neurodiversity is helpful. These conversations can take place in schools, workplaces, and community centers, providing opportunities for people to learn from one another and challenge preconceived notions. Supporting inclusive media representation is equally important. Media plays a powerful role in shaping public perceptions, and inclusive representation ensures that neurodiverse individuals are seen and heard. This involves not only featuring neurodivergent characters in film, television, and literature but also ensuring that their stories are told authentically and respectfully.

As we explore these facets of celebrating neurodiversity, it becomes clear that each effort contributes to a broader tapestry of acceptance and understanding. By amplifying diverse voices, creating events that engage and educate, and nurturing a culture that values differences, we build a world where neurodiversity is not just acknowledged but celebrated. This approach enriches our communities and enhances our collective humanity, paving the way for a future where every individual can thrive in their authenticity. As we continue to embrace these principles, let us carry forward the momentum of celebration and acceptance, ensuring that our efforts resonate not just today but in the years to come.

In the next chapter, we will delve into practical daily living skills, drawing connections between advocating for oneself and navigating everyday tasks with greater ease and confidence. As we move forward, remember that celebrating neurodiversity is a continuous journey, one that requires commitment, empathy, and a willingness to learn and grow.

NINE

EMBRACING NEURODIVERSITY IN A NEUROTYPICAL WORLD

W hen I met Cheyenne, a software developer with a remarkable ability to see patterns others missed, she shared how her attention to detail not only made her a valuable team member but also allowed her to find joy in the intricacies of code. Her story illustrates a common theme among autistic individuals: the unique strengths that can transform challenges into assets. These abilities often include analytical thinking, creativity, and an unparalleled attention to detail. Such strengths are not just personal victories but also contributions to society that deserve recognition and celebration. By focusing on these positive traits, we can begin to understand the value that neurodiversity brings to every facet of life.

9.1 STRENGTH BASED APPROACH

Historically, autism has been viewed through a deficit-based lens, emphasizing what individuals may lack rather than what they offer. This perspective neglects the rich tapestry of talents that many autistic individuals possess. Research and personal accounts show that when we shift to a strength-based approach, we uncover a wealth of abilities that can lead to success across various fields. For instance, many renowned figures, from Albert Einstein to Tim Burton, have demonstrated that autism can be a source of profound insight and innovation. These success stories challenge the conventional narrative and highlight the importance of recognizing and nurturing individual strengths. By focusing on capabilities rather than limitations, we can create environments where autistic individuals thrive.

Celebrating and using these strengths as a foundation for personal growth leads to greater self-confidence among autistic adults. Building a personal strengths inventory can be a transformative exercise. It involves identifying areas where you excel and acknowledging the value of these abilities. Participating in skill-building workshops can further enhance these strengths, providing opportunities to refine and expand your talents. For example, if you have a knack for detail-oriented tasks, a seminar in data analysis or design might help you channel this strength into a fulfilling career. By focusing on what you can do rather than what you can't, you build a sense of self-worth and confidence that propels you forward.

Leveraging your strengths in daily life can transform how you approach challenges. Analytical thinking, for instance, is invaluable in problem-solving scenarios. Whether you're tackling a complex project at work or organizing your home, your ability to break down tasks and find logical solutions can be a significant asset. Creativity and innovation can enhance team dynamics, offering fresh perspectives that inspire and engage others. Your unique insights might lead to breakthroughs that wouldn't be possible otherwise. These strengths can be applied in countless ways, from improving efficiency in daily tasks to aiding collaboration in group settings. Recognizing and utilizing your abilities not only enriches your life but also contributes to the broader community, showcasing the profound impact of embracing neurodiversity.

Strengths Inventory Exercise

Creating a personal strengths inventory can help you identify and harness your strengths. List activities where you feel confident and fulfilled. Reflect on feedback from others about your skills or qualities they admire. Use this inventory to set goals that align with your strengths, ensuring your personal and professional pursuits are fulfilling and aligned with your abilities.

9.2 UNDERSTANDING NEUROTYPICAL PERSPECTIVES

In a world designed around neurotypical norms, understanding these unwritten rules can feel like deciphering a foreign language. Social conventions often rely on such things as maintaining eye contact and interpreting subtle body language. These norms dictate the rhythm of conversations and set expectations for social behavior. Non-verbal cues, like a nod or a smile, convey agreement or friendliness, while averted eyes might suggest discomfort. For autistic individuals, these cues may not be intuitive, leading to potential misunderstandings. Recognizing these norms can help you navigate social settings with greater ease, offering insights into neurotypical expectations that might otherwise go unnoticed. This awareness doesn't require conforming to these norms, but knowing what they are can enhance your ability to engage in social situations more comfortably.

Building empathy for neurotypical experiences involves more than observing behaviors; it means actively engaging with others to understand their perspectives. Active listening exercises can be a valuable tool in this process. By focusing intently on what someone is saying, you show respect and interest, fostering mutual understanding. Participating in mixed-neurotype dialogue groups can further deepen this empathy. These groups provide a platform for sharing experiences and learning from one another. Engaging in such dialogues allows you to hear firsthand accounts of neurotypical experiences, bridging gaps in understanding and fostering a sense of community. This shared experience helps dismantle barriers, replacing them with empathy and respect, which are vital for any meaningful interaction.

Misunderstandings between neurotypical and autistic individuals often arise from differences in communication styles. Neurotypical people may interpret direct communication as bluntness, while indirect cues can be confusing for autistic individuals. These misunderstandings can lead to feelings of exclusion or frustration on both sides. By acknowledging these differences, you can begin to identify common ground. Recognizing that misinterpretations are not personal failures but natural outcomes of differing perspectives can reduce tension and encourage patience. This acknowledgment opens the door to more thoughtful and inclusive communication, where both parties feel heard and respected.

Bridging the gap between neurodiverse and neurotypical perspectives involves more than understanding; it requires action. Encouraging open dialogue and feedback is a powerful strategy. Creating spaces where questions and clarifications are welcomed helps everyone feel comfortable expressing themselves. This openness can lead to shared experiences and collaborations, enriching both parties. Activities that bring together neurodiverse and neurotypical individuals, such as community projects or collaborative workshops, promote mutual respect and understanding. These interactions help lead to a culture of inclusion, where differences are celebrated and common goals are pursued. By building bridges, you contribute to a more inclusive society where diverse perspectives enhance rather than divide.

9.3 FOSTERING MUTUAL UNDERSTANDING AND RESPECT

Fostering mutual understanding begins with creating spaces where open dialogue is the norm. Imagine a room where everyone feels safe to voice their thoughts, knowing their perspectives will be valued. Establishing ground rules is key. These guidelines ensure that conversations remain respectful and inclusive, encouraging participants to listen actively and speak empathetically. Setting these expectations helps build a foundation of trust, allowing individuals to express their unique viewpoints without fear of judgment. Hosting inclusive discussion panels can further support this environment. By bringing together diverse voices, these panels provide a platform for sharing experiences and insights, promoting a richer dialogue that bridges gaps in understanding. These discussions can also challenge stereotypes, contributing to a culture where differences are not just accepted but celebrated.

Active listening is a powerful tool for enhancing understanding. It's more than just hearing words; it's about engaging with the speaker's perspective. Reflective listening exercises can help you practice this skill. By repeating back what you've heard in your own words, you demonstrate that you've truly understood the speaker, which encourages further sharing. Paraphrasing and summarizing techniques can also enhance this process. These methods show that you're not only paying attention but also processing and valuing the information being shared. When you practice active listening, you help create an environment where everyone feels heard and respected, paving the way for deeper connections and mutual respect.

Embracing diverse perspectives enriches any setting. When people from different backgrounds and experiences come together, creativity and problem-solving are significantly enhanced. Each person brings a unique viewpoint, offering solutions and ideas that might not have been considered otherwise. This diversity of thought can lead to innovative approaches and breakthroughs, benefiting the whole group. Moreover, embracing these perspectives builds stronger, more cohesive communities. When everyone feels valued and included, collaboration naturally improves, creating a sense of belonging and unity. These communities are resilient, able to adapt, and thrive in the face of challenges because they draw strength from their diversity. This approach not only enriches group dynamics but also strengthens bonds within the community.

Incorporating diversity training into organizations and communities is an effective way to formalize these practices. Workshops focused on neurodiversity awareness can provide invaluable insights into the experiences and needs of autistic individuals. These sessions should encourage participants to explore their assumptions and biases, fostering a more inclusive mindset. Collaborative learning sessions can also be beneficial. By working together on projects or discussions, participants can experience firsthand the value of diverse perspectives. These trainings should aim to create lasting change by equipping individuals with the tools and understanding necessary to support a diverse environment. Through these efforts, organizations can cultivate a culture of inclusion and respect, ensuring that all members feel valued and empowered.

9.4 BUILDING RESILIENCE IN A NEUROTYPICAL WORLD

Resilience is the ability to adapt and bounce back from challenges, a crucial trait for navigating a world often not designed with autism in mind. For autistic individuals, resilience means finding ways to thrive despite the pressures of conforming to neurotypical norms. Resilient people show flexibility, determination, and the ability to learn from experiences. They also maintain a sense of self-worth even in adversity. This quality is vital for anyone who faces the constant negotiation between personal needs and external expectations. It provides the strength to face each day with confidence, knowing that setbacks are part of growth rather than defining failures.

Developing coping strategies is essential for building resilience. Mindfulness is a powerful tool in this regard, offering a way to manage stress by focusing on the present moment without judgment. Practicing mindfulness can help you stay grounded, reduce anxiety, and enhance emotional regulation. Positive reframing is another helpful technique. This involves viewing setbacks as opportunities for learning rather than insurmountable obstacles. By changing your perspective, you transform challenges into stepping stones for personal development. For instance, a difficult social interaction might be seen as a chance to refine communication skills rather than a defeat. These strategies build a resilient mindset, enabling you to face life's ups and downs with greater ease.

Learning from adversity is a key aspect of resilience. Each challenge carries a lesson, offering insights into your strengths and areas for growth. Reflecting on past experiences allows you to identify patterns and learn what works best for you in overcoming difficulties. Setting achievable goals is crucial here. By breaking larger objectives into smaller, more manageable steps, you create a clear path forward. This approach not only builds confidence but also encourages continuous progress. As you achieve each goal, you gain momentum, reinforcing your resilience and capacity for handling future challenges. This cycle of reflection and goal-setting builds a proactive attitude, turning adversity into a catalyst for growth.

Support networks are invaluable in building resilience. Identifying supportive allies, such as friends, family, or colleagues, provides a foundation of understanding and encouragement. These individuals offer a safe space where you can share experiences and seek advice without fear of judgment. Engaging with mentoring programs can also be beneficial. Mentors who have navigated similar challenges provide guidance and perspective, helping you see beyond immediate difficulties. They can offer strategies and resources tailored to your needs, enhancing your ability to cope effectively. By cultivating a network of support, you create a web of connections that bolster your resilience, ensuring that you never face challenges alone. This network not only supports you in times of need but also celebrates your successes, reinforcing the belief that you can overcome any obstacle life presents.

9.5 SHARING YOUR STORY: IMPACT AND EMPOWERMENT

Stories hold immense power. They connect us, bridging gaps that facts alone cannot. For autistic individuals, sharing personal narratives can illuminate the often misunderstood facets of autism, fostering empathy and awareness. When you share your story, you invite others to see the world through your eyes. This act of storytelling not only raises awareness but also empowers others who may feel isolated in their experiences. It is through these shared narratives that we inspire change, challenge stereotypes, and build communities rooted in understanding. Your story, with its unique struggles and triumphs, has the potential to resonate deeply with others, offering them a sense of belonging and hope.

Crafting your narrative requires reflection and intention. Begin by identifying the moments in your life that have shaped you. These may include challenges overcome, pivotal realizations, or experiences that highlight your unique perspective. Each of these moments carries a lesson that can guide others. Structure your story with your audience in mind. For some, a chronological approach works best, while others might find thematic storytelling more effective. Whether you're speaking to friends, writing a blog, or addressing a wider audience, tailor your narrative for clarity and impact. Remember, your story is not just a recounting of events but a canvas of insights that can educate and empower.

With a crafted narrative, the next step is finding the right platform to share it. Blogging is a versatile option, allowing you to reach a broad audience. Guest writing for established publications can also amplify your voice, introducing your story to readers who might not typically engage with autism-related content. Public speaking events and panels offer a more direct connection, where you can engage with your audience in real time. These platforms not only amplify your story but also position you as an advocate for neurodiversity. By choosing the right medium, you ensure your message reaches those who need to hear it most.

Sharing your personal story can feel daunting, especially when faced with vulnerability fears. These fears are natural but can be managed with practice and focus. Start small by sharing with trusted friends or in supportive online groups. This practice builds your confidence, allowing you to expand your audience gradually. Focus on the positive impact your story can have. Remind yourself that your experiences can offer support, insight, and inspiration to others. This focus shifts attention from your fears to the potential good your narrative can do. Remember, each time you share, you contribute to a broader understanding of autism, helping to build a world where neurodiversity is celebrated and embraced.

9.6 ENCOURAGING NEURODIVERSITY IN FUTURE GENERATIONS

Educating young people about neurodiversity from an early age is vital for fostering acceptance and understanding. By incorporating neurodiversity into educational curriculums, we can create environments where children learn to embrace differences as natural and valuable. Schools should weave neurodiversity into lessons across subjects, making it a regular part of classroom discussions. This approach helps students see the world through a lens of inclusivity, encouraging them to appreciate the diverse ways people think and learn. Promoting neurodiversity in school programs goes beyond just awareness; it involves celebrating the unique strengths each student brings. Teachers can introduce activities that highlight various learning styles, helping students recognize and respect the different ways their peers experience the world.

Parents and educators play crucial roles in encouraging neurodiversity. At home, parents can encourage open discussions about differences, using books or media that portray diverse characters and experiences. These conversations help children understand that being different is not only okay but also something to celebrate. Providing resources and support is equally important. Parents should seek materials that educate both themselves and their children about neurodiversity, ensuring they have the knowledge to support their child's development. Educators have a responsibility to create classrooms that reflect a commitment to inclusivity. They can do this by integrating diverse teaching methods that cater to a range of learning preferences so that all students feel supported and valued.

Creating inclusive learning environments for future generations requires intentional strategies. Implementing universal design in classrooms can make a significant difference. This approach involves designing spaces and lessons that are accessible to everyone, regardless of their abilities or learning styles. For example, providing materials in multiple formats—such as visual, auditory, and tactile—ensures all students can engage with the content. Encouraging peer support and collaboration is another effective strategy. Group activities where students work together on projects allow them to learn from each other's strengths and perspectives. Such collaboration builds a community of learners who appreciate and leverage their diversity.

Celebrating neurodiverse achievements in educational settings is essential for fostering an environment of acceptance and pride. Schools can showcase diverse role models, highlighting individuals who have made significant contributions despite—or because of—their neurodiversity. Hosting recognition events and ceremonies that celebrate these achievements sends a powerful message to all students: that their unique qualities are to be valued and honored. These events provide opportunities for students to share their stories and talents with the broader community, promoting a culture of inclusivity and respect. By recognizing and celebrating these achievements, we inspire future generations to embrace their identities and pursue their passions with confidence.

9.7 LIVING UNMASKED: A JOURNEY TO AUTHENTICITY

Living authentically means shedding the layers of pretense and embracing who you truly are. This process is both challenging and rewarding. For those who have spent years conforming to societal expectations, the idea of unmasking can feel daunting. Yet, it's through this unmasking that you find freedom. Authenticity allows you to align your actions with your values, reducing the internal conflict that comes from pretending to be someone you're not. It opens the door to genuine connections and a deeper understanding of yourself. It is important to understand that giving up these masking behaviors does not happen overnight. It is an incremental process, and you need to be kind to yourself and applaud your efforts. While the path to authenticity may be paved with uncertainty, the rewards are profound, including greater self-awareness, inner peace, and meaningful relationships.

Living authentically involves accepting and embracing vulnerability. Vulnerability involves accepting imperfections and uncertainties and acknowledging that it's okay not to have all the answers. This acceptance is liberating. It allows you to show up as you are without the fear of judgment or rejection. Sharing your authentic experiences with others can strengthen bonds and create empathy. When you allow yourself to be vulnerable, you invite others to do the same, creating a space where genuine connections can flourish. This reciprocal openness can transform relationships, turning them into supportive environments where everyone feels seen and valued. Vulnerability, though often perceived as a weakness, is a source of strength that leads to resilience and authenticity.

Creating safe spaces for authenticity is essential in this process. These spaces are built on trust and openness, where you feel comfortable expressing yourself without fear of judgment. Establishing trust in relationships requires honesty and consistency. When you communicate openly and listen actively, you lay the groundwork for a supportive environment. Encouraging self-expression involves respecting diverse perspectives and allowing others to share their truths. In these spaces, authenticity is not only accepted but celebrated. They become sanctuaries where you can explore your identity, try new things, and learn from mistakes without the pressure to conform. By fostering such environments, you empower yourself and others to live authentically, enriching your interactions and strengthening your community.

The stories of individuals who have embraced authenticity serve as powerful inspiration. Consider Thuong, who, after years of masking his true self, decided to openly share his love for painting, a passion he had kept hidden for fear of ridicule. By doing so, he not only found immense personal joy but also connected with others who shared his interest. Through these connections, he discovered a community that valued him for who he was, not who he pretended to be. His journey illustrates the profound impact of living authentically. The lessons learned from such experiences highlight the importance of embracing your true self despite the challenges. Authenticity fosters a life filled with purpose and connection, where you can thrive as you are.

9.8 THE FUTURE OF AUTISM: ADVOCACY AND INNOVATION

As we look toward the horizon, the landscape of autism advocacy and research is evolving in exciting ways. Advances in assistive technology are transforming how autistic individuals interact with the world. Devices that enhance communication and facilitate learning are becoming more sophisticated and accessible. For instance, apps tailored to promote social skills or manage sensory overload are now widely available. These tools not only support daily living but also empower individuals to express themselves more fully. Simultaneously, new approaches to autism support are emerging. These approaches prioritize personalized strategies that respect individual differences, moving away from one-size-fits-all solutions. This shift reflects a deeper understanding of autism as a spectrum, where each person's needs are unique and deserving of tailored support.

Innovations in neurodiversity advocacy are also making significant strides. Inclusive policy development is gaining momentum, driven by a growing recognition of the value that neurodiverse individuals bring to workplaces and communities. Policies that promote accessibility and inclusion are no longer just ethical imperatives; they are seen as beneficial to society as a whole. Technological solutions are playing a crucial role in this transformation. From software that facilitates remote work to platforms that streamline accessibility in public spaces, technology is bridging gaps that once seemed insurmountable. These advancements ensure that environments are not just accommodating but are actively welcoming to all forms of diversity, including neurodiversity. By leveraging these innovations, we can build a world that celebrates differences and harnesses them for collective growth.

Collaboration is essential to creating positive change. Partnerships between researchers, practitioners, and those with lived experience of autism are creating a more holistic approach to advocacy. By working together, these stakeholders can develop strategies that are informed by both scientific insight and real-world application. Engaging with policymakers and advocates is another crucial element. By bringing the voices of autistic individuals to the forefront of legislative discussions, we ensure that policies reflect the needs and aspirations of the community. This engagement is vital for creating systems that are not only inclusive but also empowering, allowing autistic individuals to participate fully and authentically in society.

Imagining a future where neurodiversity is fully embraced and celebrated is not just a dream; it is a vision grounded in possibility. Inclusive communities are those where every individual's contributions are valued and where differences are seen as strengths rather than obstacles. Supporting lifelong learning and development is key to realizing this vision. By providing opportunities for continuous education and growth, we nurture a society that thrives on diversity of thought and experience. This commitment to lifelong learning ensures that everyone, regardless of neurotype, has the chance to develop their skills and pursue their passions. As we look forward, the path is clear: by embracing innovation, encouraging collaboration, and championing inclusion, we can create a world where neurodiversity is celebrated as an integral part of the human experience.

CONCLUSION

As we reach the end of our journey together, let's take a moment to reflect on the key themes and strategies we've explored. This book has offered practical tools and insights aimed at empowering you to live authentically and thrive without the need for masking. We've delved into the complexities of executive functioning, sensory management, and communication, providing you with strategies to navigate these challenges effectively.

Throughout this book, I have aimed to reaffirm a vision of empowerment for autistic adults. It is about embracing your unique traits and viewing them as strengths rather than limitations. By celebrating neurodiversity, we can begin to see the profound value that each individual brings to the landscape of society. Your unique cognitive style is not just valid; it is vital and enriching.

One of the core messages has been the importance of practical tools. These tools help you manage everyday tasks, communicate your needs clearly, and create environments that support your well-being. Whether it's organizing your daily schedule, planning meals that suit your sensory preferences, or advocating for yourself at work, these strategies are designed to enhance your quality of life.

Now, more than ever, it's crucial to celebrate neurodiversity. Embrace who you are with all your strengths and challenges. Remember, the world needs your perspective and talents. By understanding and leveraging your unique abilities, you contribute not only to your personal growth but also to the collective advancement of society.

I urge you to take the insights and tools provided here and use them to advocate for yourself and others. Self-advocacy is a powerful tool that can lead to greater independence and empowerment. As you navigate the world, remember that your voice matters and your experiences are valuable. Advocate for the changes you wish to see in your community and beyond.

Engaging with your community is another vital step. Building supportive networks can provide you with strength and encouragement. Participate in advocacy and awareness efforts to nurture understanding and inclusivity. By connecting with others, you can create a ripple effect of change, promoting a more inclusive and accepting world.

The journey of self-discovery and growth does not end here. Lifelong learning is essential for continuous personal development. Keep exploring new strategies and tools to thrive in various aspects of your life. Every day presents new opportunities to learn and grow.

I want to express my heartfelt gratitude for allowing me to accompany you on this journey. Your willingness to explore, learn, and grow is truly inspiring. I hope that the insights and tools shared in this book empower you to live a life that is true to yourself.

I invite you to share your experiences and connect with others through the resources and community platforms provided. Your feedback is invaluable and can help others who are on similar paths. By sharing your journey, you contribute to a larger community of support and understanding.

As you continue forward, remember that living unmasked is a journey filled with potential and promise. Embrace it with confidence and courage. You have the power to thrive in a world that is increasingly recognizing the strengths of neurodiversity. May your path be filled with authenticity, joy, and connection.

KEEPING THE MOMENTUM ALIVE

Now that you've explored tools and strategies to thrive as your authentic self, it's time to share what you've gained with others.

By leaving your honest opinion of **Living with Adult Autism** on the platform where you purchased the book, you can guide other autistic adults and their allies toward the support and understanding they're looking for.

Your review doesn't just help potential readers—it helps keep the conversation about neurodiversity alive. When we share our experiences, we create a world that values authenticity, acceptance, and growth.

Thank you for being part of this journey. Together, we can inspire others to embrace their strengths and live fully as they are.

Your words have the power to make an impact. Let's keep the momentum alive.

Warmly,
Claude Moore

REFERENCES

Attwood and Garnett Events. (n.d.). *Experiences of adults diagnosed autistic later in life.* Retrieved from https://attwoodandgarnettevents.com/experiences-of-adults-diagnosed-autistic-later-in-life/

Neurodiversity Network. (n.d.). *Neurodiverse advocates leaders.* Retrieved from https://www.neurodiversitynetwork.net/neurodivergent-leaders

Healthline. (n.d.). *Understanding autism masking and its consequences.* Retrieved from https://www.healthline.com/health/autism/autism-masking

PMC. (n.d.). *Intersectionality within critical autism studies: A narrative.* Retrieved from https://pmc.ncbi.nlm.nih.gov/articles/PMC9908281/

National Autistic Society. (n.d.). *Sensory differences - a guide for all audiences.* Retrieved from https://www.autism.org.uk/advice-and-guidance/topics/sensory-differences/sensory-differences/all-audiences

Hands Center. (n.d.). *9 sensory-friendly home modifications for autism.* Retrieved from https://www.handscenter.com/9-sensory-friendly-home-modifications-for-autism

ABA Centers. (n.d.). *Managing sensory issues in the workplace: Careers with ASD.* Retrieved from https://www.abacenters.com/sensory-issues-in-the-workplace/

Maple Community. (n.d.). *Assistive technology for autism.* Retrieved from https://maplecommunity.com.au/disability-support-services/autism-support-care/assistive-technology-for-autism/

Autism Spectrum News. (n.d.). *Three strategies to strengthen communication for adults with autism and learning differences.* Retrieved from https://autismspectrumnews.org/three-strategies-to-strengthen-communication-for-adults-with-autism-and-learning-differences/

ABTABA. (n.d.). *Social skills training for autism spectrum disorder.* Retrieved from https://www.abtaba.com/blog/social-skills-training

National Autistic Society. (n.d.). *Making friends - a guide for autistic adults.* Retrieved from https://www.autism.org.uk/advice-and-guidance/topics/family-life-and-relationships/making-friends/autistic-adults

Autism Speaks. (n.d.). *Dating tips for autistic adults.* Retrieved from https://www.autismspeaks.org/expert-opinion/dating

Workology. (n.d.). *27 companies who hire adults with autism.* Retrieved from https://workology.com/companies-hiring-adults-with-autism/

ADA National Network. (n.d.). *Reasonable accommodations in the workplace*. Retrieved from https://adata.org/factsheet/reasonable-accommodations-workplace

Life Skills Advocate. (n.d.). *10 powerful tools for jumpstarting executive functioning in 2023*. Retrieved from https://lifeskillsadvocate.com/blog/10-powerful-tools-for-jumpstarting-executive-functioning-in-2023/

Enna. (n.d.). *The benefits of flexible work arrangements for neurodivergent employees*. Retrieved from https://enna.org/the-benefits-of-flexible-work-arrangements-for-neurodivergent-employees/

PMC. (n.d.). *Mindfulness-based stress reduction for autistic adults*. Retrieved from https://pmc.ncbi.nlm.nih.gov/articles/PMC10851647/

Autism Speaks. (n.d.). *Autism and anxiety in adults*. Retrieved from https://www.autismspeaks.org/blog/autism-and-anxiety-adults

Well+Good. (n.d.). *7 autism self-care tips that are actually effective*. Retrieved from https://www.wellandgood.com/self-care-autism/

ABA Centers FL. (n.d.). *Art therapy for autism: 8 incredible benefits*. Retrieved from https://abacentersfl.com/blog/art-therapy-for-autism/

Autistic Self Advocacy Network. (n.d.). *Autistic self advocacy network*. Retrieved from https://autisticadvocacy.org/

Autism Speaks. (n.d.). *Finding your community*. Retrieved from https://www.autism-speaks.org/finding-your-community

Reframing Autism. (n.d.). *Autism advocacy: A reflection on my journey and tips for newcomers*. Retrieved from https://reframingautism.org.au/autism-advocacy-a-reflection-on-my-journey-and-tips-for-newcomers/

CDC. (n.d.). *Accessing services for autism spectrum disorder*. Retrieved from https://www.cdc.gov/autism/treatment/accessing-services.html

Autism Society of Minnesota. (n.d.). *Executive function resources*. Retrieved from https://ausm.org/ausm-resources/executive-function-resources/

Level Ahead ABA. (n.d.). *Easy autism-friendly recipes for adults*. Retrieved from https://www.levelaheadaba.com/blog/autism-friendly-recipes-for-adults

Forbes Advisor. (2024). *Best budgeting apps of November 2024*. Retrieved from https://www.forbes.com/advisor/banking/best-budgeting-apps/

Dream Big Children. (n.d.). *Traveling with autism: 10 essential tips for stress-free trips*. Retrieved from https://dreambigchildren.com/blog/traveling-with-autism-10-essential-tips-for-stress-free-trips/

Relational Psych Group. (n.d.). *Self-advocacy strategies for neurodivergent adults*. Retrieved from https://www.relationalpsych.group/articles/self-advocacy-strategies-for-neurodivergent-adults

Autism Awareness Centre. (n.d.). *Community inclusion for autistic people: Ideas and options*. Retrieved from https://autismawarenesscentre.com/community-inclusion-for-autistic-people-ideas-and-options/

Neurodiverging. (n.d.). *The societal impact of neurodiversity: Embracing differences for a better future*. Retrieved from https://www.neurodiverging.com/the-societal-impact-of-neurodiversity-embracing-differences-for-a-better-future/

Autism Speaks. (n.d.). *Advocacy tool kit*. Retrieved from https://www.autismspeaks.org/tool-kit/advocacy-tool-kit

Harvard Health Blog. (2017). *A strengths-based approach to autism*. Retrieved from https://www.health.harvard.edu/blog/a-strength-focused-approach-to-autism-2017042011607

IRL Social Skills. (n.d.). *How social norms impact autistic and neurodivergent people*. Retrieved from https://www.irlsocialskills.com/blog-post-archive/how-social-norms-impact-autistic-and-neurodivergent-people

Forbes. (2022). *Rivera's workplace neurodiversity rising: Trend for 2023*. Retrieved from https://www.forbes.com/sites/drnancydoyle/2022/12/19/riveras-workplace-neurodiversity-rising-trend-for-2023/

Behavioral Innovations. (n.d.). *20 famous people with autism spectrum disorder (ASD)*. Retrieved from https://behavioral-innovations.com/blog/20-famous-people-with-autism-spectrum-disorder-asd/